EVERYBODY'S KNIFE BIBLE

by

DonPaul

*All new ways to use and enjoy
your knives in the great outdoors.*

3rd Edition
Revised, expanded and illustrated

<u>**Includes**</u>: Special instruction on self defense.for women.
Latest sharpening tips to make
your knife cut like a razor.

Photography: T McLaughlin et al
Cover Design: Sunny Woods Paul

WHY WE USE "BIBLE"
IN OUR TITLE

After reading my Bible, I'm convinced. It's the inspired Word of our Creator, and it teaches men and women how to live successfully—-in right relationship to others and to God. The founders of my country believed that too. This book teaches you how to get along in the outdoors successfully with your knife in right relationship with others and Nature, so I called it a bible. But this book doesn't even come close to doing for knives what the real Bible does for people. Read the real Bible; you'll see what I mean.

© Don Paul and Path Finder. *Wir sprechen auch Deutsch, und haben es vor, dieses Buch zu übersetsen. Tambien hablamos Espanol , y lo vamos a traducir.*

PUBLISHER'S CATALOGING IN PUBLICATION

Paul, Don 1937---
      Everybody's Knife Bible, the all-new way to use and enjoy your knives in the great outdoors. / by Don Paul. 3rd Edition.
      Includes index.
      ISBN: 0-938263-13-7
      1. Woodcraft, outdoors. 2. Craftsmanship, outdoors, Guide-books.
      3. Outdoor Sports. I. Title. II. Title: Everybody's Knife Bible.
III. Use your knives in the outdoors.
      PN147.P3 1992   796.042
                                          GV191.7.P38.1992

      Library of Congress Catalog Number: LC 92-80509

      ISBN 0-938263-13-7

Path Finder Publications
1296 E. Gibson Suite E-301, Woodland, Calif 95695

INTRODUCING...

OUTDOOR BOOKS by
PATH FINDER PUBLICATIONS
New method books for outdoors people.

Once you own any of our books, you can get a new, updated copy for half price, no matter why. If your book drowns or gets eaten by a goat, send us what's left of your old copy. (we'll pay postage on the new one) Even if you need to use the pages to make a fire in the woods, save a few burnt offerings and get back to us.

Path Finder began over 10 years ago. We first invented a way never to get lost in the woods without using a map; it's called, _The Green Beret's Compass Course, Never Get lost._ Over 25,000 copies are in print.

Next, we added to our book list and widened our distribution. We published:

> _Everybody's Outdoor Survival Guide_
> _Great Livin' in Grubby Times_
> _24 + Ways to Use Your Hammock in the Field._

We develop and write about all kinds of new ideas and outdoor methods. We're the innovative people who wrote about:

√A 30¢ two ounce wilderness bed for sleeping above ground.

√The modification for your hunting knife sheath which enables you to see the floor of a jungle at night.

√A new shooting system to give you super bullet placement, day or night.

√Escape and evasion, taught by an honor Army Ranger Grad.

√Life saving, simple procedures for self defense.

√Terrain analysis for saving energy as you travel on foot over rough country.

√A new cold-weather survival method to keep you alive anywhere.

√A guide to water purification for any survivalist.

I

√How to use animals to double your survive-ability.
√Wind reading for super long distance shooting.
√Green Beret team concepts applied to survival groups so you can enjoy the ultimate life-style outdoors.

All of our books have gone into multiple editions. Most major outdoor magazines have reviewed our books and our systems have been adopted by many outdoor organizations. We've been represented by over 500 dealers and we've supplied our books by mail order to outdoorsmen from all over the world.

We use independent editors and electronic manuscript scrubbers to make our books quick readers. Pictures and illustrations make our concepts easy to understand. We're care about saving your time.

We just don't want to publish words; we want to supply the newest, most innovative information we can. Hopefully, that's what we did in this book.

We plan to publish *AMMO FOREVER,* a simplified reloading guide for survivalists, *THE COMPLETE SELF DEFENSE MANUAL* and a second *EVERYBODY'S KNIFE BIBLE (BOOK II)* featuring over a hundred ways to use your knives during 1992.

(See the order coupons in the back of this book.)

> **HANG ON NOW, AND LET US SHOW YOU HOW TO USE YOUR MOST BASIC OUTDOOR TOOLS---YOUR INDISPENSABLE KNIVES**

EVERYBODY'S KNIFE BIBLE

3rd Edition

CONTENTS

<u>INTRODUCTION:</u> **Why a new knife bible?** Knives need improvement. Here's how to improve yours, bring it into the future, and let it lead you through the woods.

INTRODUCTION

WHY A NEW KNIFE BIBLE?

Because today's knives don't do nearly as much as they could and new discoveries in manufacture are newsworthy.

With manufacturers' legal liability making them nail-biting nervous, and with government agencies writing regulations that slow down and impede American production, it doesn't look like we'll see a change in the future. Getting high field performance out of your knives will have to be a do-it-yourself affair.

This is a book about improvement, expansion and new uses in the field of knives. It will make you better than average in the outdoors with a knife. When you read this book, you'll be able to take your knife—any knife, and modify it with unbelievable changes. Your knives will become unique and you'll know how to put them to best use. Pictures and graphic illustrations make this a **quick-reader**. Very few of us have time to dig through complicated pages.

1

I wrote this book because I've learned enough to produce what might be landmark knowledge about knives. Some friends spent a lot of time with me in the field using these things, and we discovered:

**Compared to what knives should do,
today's knives don't.**

That's too bad. Of all the things you carry into the field with you, your knife is one of the most basic. If it only cuts and slices for you, you're missing a lot of your knife's potential.

Do the people I consulted really know what a knife should do? When a person spends his life working in the woods and jungles of the world, he learns a lot more about knives than the people who sit at desks and design them. It's not that we have an axe to grind (no pun). It's just that we've used these things so long and so often that we are acutely aware of what a knife ought to do—-but won't.

What's the reason for modern knives' complete failure to do so many tricks in the woods and jungle? American manufacturers can no longer be as creative as our ancestors. Even though we might know more, we produce less. Many government officials have **no concept of the value of time** because they have found the great eternal resting place, (their job). To us who produce, time is money; to them, a waste of time means money. Therefore, they write counter-productive regulations and slow down our progress.

Moreover, broadening the use of any product sometimes increases the chance of injury to the user. The company's insurers get nervous; the rates increase. As soon as product liability insurance goes up, the end product becomes costlier and therefore can't compete. In the case of knives, manufacturers can't think about a knife cutting down a tree; that's too risky. Making a knife to get you across a river safely or measure rapelling rope for you could likewise be legally troublesome.

The shortcomings of today's knives can be fixed. But the manufacturers in this country are not about to pioneer anything which could end up in a courtroom. Would you? Even if you would be so bold as to manufacture anything in this country, at all, would you add to the risk by getting creative?

2

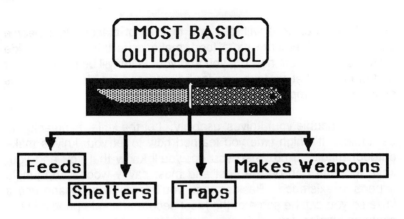

MOST BASIC OUTDOOR TOOL

Feeds

Shelters **Traps**

Makes Weapons

If you want your knife to do better, **you** fix it. You can make your knife adapt to you—your special outdoor needs, your abilities, and even some wierd uses. You can borrow our ideas—ideas that came about because we sliced, slaughtered, and survived our way out of half the jungles in the world.

We wish you had been with us; probably you do too. But we'll make the best of a lonesome situation and let you borrow from our experience.

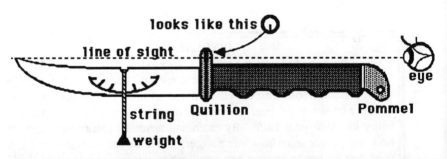

looks like this

line of sight

string   Quillion   Pommel

weight

eye

One of the many modifications found throughout this book. You'll be able to do dozens of new outdoor tricks with your knife. Note hole in pommel, for example. The hole in the pommel allows you to pull your knife out of anything with a force more than twenty times greater than you could by only gripping the handle. Similar hole in quillion makes knife a sighting device.

Now, your knife will take you to a lot of places other people can't go. It will procure more food, make more things and provide more comfort. From now on, you and your knife will be surer, trickier and craftier. Let us take you far beyond and far above what has ever been accomplished before with this ancient tool.

Let's double your knives' usability. Let the knife manufacturers be afraid. It's high time you learned how to let your knives make outdoor magic. And when you do, you'll know that you and your knife together can be the best and most savvy woods and jungle experts in existence. Besides that, you'll learn to carry and use a knife so you can be some of the most secure and safe people in our concrete jungles, too...

Speaking of concrete jungles... Few things are more attractive to a thief than a knife. Plan on keeping your knife for life. Take the time to inscribe your tang (softer metal) with your I.D. number.

DISCLAIMER
On behalf of you, the reader, I wish to thank the framers of our Constitution of giving us the right of free speech. Because of that, I can write a book about knives which dares to take you beyond what ordinary knives do for you. I wrote this because I wanted you to have a better life with your knife. By extending anyone's ability anywhere, however, there may be some danger. Neither the author nor the publisher wishes to assume any liability for any use or misuse of the information in this book. Oh—-and one more thing—-like the old Sarge on the TV Series, *Hill St Blues* always told us: "Let's be careful out there."

Penlight on blade lights up your night life in the woods.

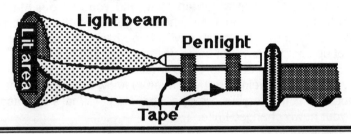

Light beam

Penlight

Lit area

Tape

Night work is so much easier with the cutting area illuminated. Light should be in handle and shine through quillion. But why wait? Become a woods pro now! You can fix up your own knife with this and loads of other features in this book.

Chapter 1

CONVERTING YOUR KNIFE INTO A SUPER OUTDOOR TOOL

Utility to weight ratio is a concept we came up with when we researched and wrote *24+ WAYS TO USE YOUR HAMMOCK IN THE FIELD.* We were looking for a phrase to describe a ratio of multiple uses on an outdoor item to its weight. The higher the ratio, the better the item for survival.

The more things weigh, the more horse or human-power is required to move them. Also, if every item you need in the outdoors only has one use, you'll need to carry a lot of items.

Whether you're gas-powered mobile or you go into the woods on foot, you'll do better with a lighter load and fewer items. Therefore, fix all your outdoor gear so it makes multiple chore magic. Besides that, try to make each outdoor item do tricks nothing else can do for you.

That's what this chapter is about. We're going to show you how to make your sheath do some outdoor magic. More than that, we'll show you how to make your knife do stuff in the woods nobody else can do. For example:

How to tell time. That would be helpful if you have to meet somebody at 15:30 at a certain spot, and you use our mapless navigation system so you know where to go. Even more important, it's critical to know how much daylight you have left—whether you will set up camp or arrive at some destination at the right time.

Suppose you intend to climb a hill with your backpack. You know your pack's weight, but you need to know the angle of the hill so you can compute your climbing work load. What's that angle? Use your newly changed knife.

You want to fall a tree, but you are not sure how far out it will land from the stump, or whether it will bridge the ravine you need to cross. How high is the tree? Let your knife figure the distance.

You need to walk down the side of a steep mountain and use your 100 ft. rope for support. If the distance down is longer than your rope, you should learn to fly. How high is your starting point from the ground? Again, that's what your knife will tell you.

You know how high a mountain top is because it's labeled on your map. You need to know your personal elevation. How can you figure it? It's knife time.

Suppose you want to cross a river and you don't know if your rope will span the water. You also don't know how far upstream you should enter the water in order to cross safely. What's the distance across the river? Turn your knife flat, stick it into a tree, and line out the distance.

All of the above—and more can be performed by making some changes on your knife. Any old clinometers won't do; they have to be one of our design. We took all the complicated math out of the process and designed a special easy-to-use percentage guide, a protractor for angles and direction measurement, plus a quadrant for using your knife as a time piece. Just put our clinometers on your knife, and make outdoor magic.

Learn to understand the different kinds of blades available. While a high tipped, upswept blade isn't necessary, it works best for our first trick. In order to take accurate angle measurements with your knife, you need to be able to sight it like a weapon. The more accurately you sight, the more accurate will be the angles you shoot. If your own knife is a drop point version, you'll have more trouble, but you can fix it to sight accurately.

> **Modify your knife so you can aim it up and down. The clinometer plates we designed for the sides of the blade will give you lots of woods information.**

Modify your knife so you can aim it, (like a pistol). First, create the back sight. Cut a "V" notch on the top of your quillion or drill a hole. For the front sight, use the tip of the blade. If the tip can't be seen through the peep hole or v-notch, buy a shotgun bead or small sight from a gunsmith and install it on the back of the blade.

If your knife has a dropped point, put a notch on the back of the bolster (folding belt knife), or pommel (hunting knife). Then drill a hole through the quillion large enough to enable you to sight on a landmark. Later, you will be running a piece of thread (glue) from the rear sight to the front sight, because you need to install the clinometer plates with their tops parallel to the sighting line.

Next, use a triangular file, and notch the back of the blade, which will locate the center (top) of the clinometer plates. With the line of sight level, a weighted line from the new notch on the back of your blade will designate zero on the Tangent Plate, and ninety degrees (or East) on the Protractor Plate.

UNDERSTANDING YOUR CLINOMETER
AND DEGREE PLATES

To do everything you need to do in the outdoors, put all three of our plates on the sides of your knife. They are:

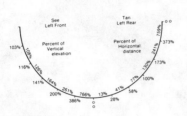

A.

A: The clinometer, which goes on the left side of your knife. That plate will measure: 1. heights of all the woods objects on the rearmost quadrant (because you will always be measuring above the horizon), and, 2. linear distances down on the foremost quadrant, (because you will always be sighting down.)

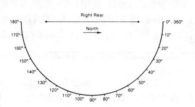

B

B: The degree wheel. It covers a complete 360º because you can easily compute back azimuths by adding 180º to the forward azimuths printed.

C: The time piece. Aim your knife at the top of the sun and the plate tells you how much time is left before dark. Since you know the time of sunset and sunrise you can easily figure the time all day long. (Aim at the **top** of the sun.)

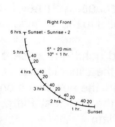

C.

Copy these clinometers on a copier, and enlarge or shrink them so they fit your knife blade. Then, cut them out and tape them on your knife. Engrave the data right through the paper. Make sure to put the Trig Function Clinometer, (A) on the left side of your blade.

Placing these on your knife correctly is important. Begin by aligning the plates' top (straight line) parallel with the line of sight. (Not the blade) Once parallel, place the center directly under and just touching the "V" notch across the back of the blade. Now, the clinometer plate is in place properly; tape it down. Once taped, double-check the alignment.

METHODS OF MODIFICATION

Use an electric engraving pencil. Trace carefully all of the information onto the sides of your knife. Use a guide (wooden ruler, or steel straight edge) to do a neat job. Note that on stainless, an engraving pencil doesn't make much of a mark. According to custom knife maker Ray Gwaltney, you can push down hard and

This is what you'll sight through when you drill the quillion and use the tip of your knife like a front rifle sight. You'll create a <u>very accurate system.</u>

make the impression much easier to read. Ray also advocates the use of a Moto-Dremel tool with a grinding stone. "Just make sure to

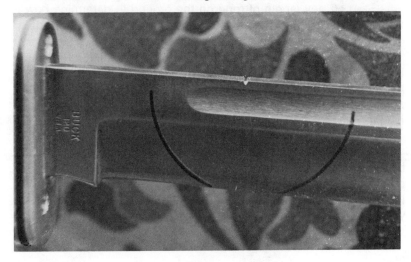

9

grind slowly," he says, "otherwise you can generate too much heat and wipe out the blade's temper."

Photocopy copy all the clinometer plates to use on a second knife. Also, this information is critical for a chainsaw. Once installed, you can aim your saw at the top of a tree and tell exactly where the tip will land after you fall it. Drill through the chainsaw's bar at the top center point of the clinometer plate. Thread a plumb line through that hole when you need it.

Plates B and C go on the right side of your blade. If your blade isn't long enough for both B and C, superimpose the two. Engrave the C plate with only the hour indications first, then engrave the B plate right over it; just remember that five degrees equals 20 minutes.

Years ago, history's scholars determined that distances should be measured in common units—first yards, feet, and now, meters and centimeters etc. In the woods, those units of measure don't work. Who carries a tape measure? Use steps. With minimal practice, you'll become consistent. With a tree, for example, count any number of the steps away from the base, then stand there. Aim your knife, multiply the indicated percentage times the number of steps you took and you determine how many steps high it is from your eyeball level.

Step off any length of rope on the ground to determine how it will relate to the rest of the measurements you'll take in the woods.

All you have to do in order to determine the height of anything is sight on it, pinch off the weighted line-indicator, and read the percentage on your clinometer scale. Then, multiply that percentage number by the distance to the object and you determine the object's height.

So, questions such as, "Where will the top land?" And "Will it bridge a river for you?" Or, "How much rope will you need to tie it off?" Are all found by stepping off the distance. Because of this, all the measuring tools you will ever need will always be with you— your legs.

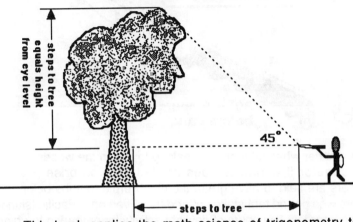

Your knife finds tree height at 45 degrees

steps to tree equals height from eye level

45°

steps to tree

This book applies the math science of trigonometry to find various heights and distances in the woods. You don't have to do that because the percentages you measure are already a computed result of a trig function. Your new clinometer is calibrated to keep things simple and easy. If you want to understand the math behind the development, any trigonometry course will lay it all out for you.

TELLING TIME WITH YOUR KNIFE

For the indicated time before sunset, read the right (C) side of your knife. We figured out a way to point your knife at the sun and tell what time it is. More critical for outdoor persons, however, is knowing how much time is left before dark.

With variations on the theme, outdoor sports people fit one of three categories: Beginners, Outdoorsmen, and Master Woodsmen.
Beginners stay on the trails, travel by day, and sleep in a camp during the night.
Outdoorsmen go off trails a lot, and navigate with map and compass during the day. At night, they generally camp.
Master outdoorsmen travel anytime, anywhere, and sleep when they feel like it. Some of these have a lot of night travel experience (military patrols abroad or night hunting). Scars on thier shins remind them to avoid it when possible.

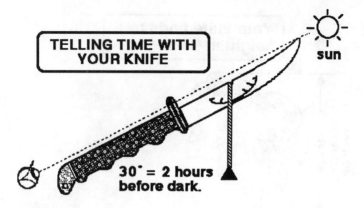

TELLING TIME WITH YOUR KNIFE

sun

30° = 2 hours before dark.

No matter what category you belong to, life in the woods will be much sweeter if darkness does not fall as a surprise. Good gardeners are said to have green thumbs. Purple thumbs belong to campers who pound tent stakes after dark. Even on a Pacific Island, you plan your last few hours of daylight activity by preparing to enjoy a good night's sleep. In cold country, however, failure to plan and prepare your camp in daylight can be disastrous. Knowing how much more daylight you have in cold climate is abso-freezing-lutely critical.

If you use the P.A.U.L. system of navigation, (*Green Beret's Compass Course*), you'll know when you should arrive at your starting point because the system converts time as it relates to how fast you travel and you don't wander all over the forest looking for a backtrail or landmark way home. The system bee-lines you the fastest way, by straight line, back to camp, base, or home.

Think about it. One day contains 24 hours; one circle contains 360 degrees. So, every hour, the sun sweeps through 15 degrees of vertical angle. Therefore, five degrees equal twenty minutes. Likewise, in a 90 degree quadrant, you have six hours of time to measure. Of course, six hours before sunset, the sun will be ninety degrees—overhead.

There's a problem. If you look directly at God's sun, you will do damage to your (only human) eyes. Wear sunglasses or make a pair of slit glasses out of tree bark. Either way, you cut down on the amount of sunlight to which your eyes are exposed.

12

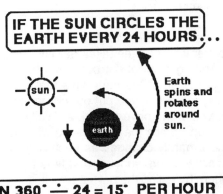

IF THE SUN CIRCLES THE EARTH EVERY 24 HOURS...

sun

earth

Earth spins and rotates around sun.

...THEN 360° ÷ 24 = 15° PER HOUR
SO, 45° IS THREE HOURS

Sight your knife on the top of the sun. Sunset refers to the time the sun disapears. The graduations on our time quadrant will tell you how much daylight you have to work with.

In the event you will be doing anything that requires full sunlight, measure the time before the sun drops behind the highest

Take care of your eyes. Don't look directly at the sun.

13

mountain. Sight on the mountain top, and then the sun. The elapsed time (on the plate) between the two measurements gives you the duration of dusk.

In the first *Crocodile Dundee*, Mick wants to impress his guest, the newspaper writer, so he takes her into the wilds of the Northern Territory. They get out of the boat, and he looks at Wally's watch, then checks the sun. He then says that it's two o'clock, and the woman is impressed. If you put our clinometer plates on the side of your knife, you won't have to look at Wally's watch before you tell time by the sun. Since the local media will publish the exact time of sunset, and it hardly changes as each day gets shorter or longer, you can shoot the sun, subtract that time from sunset, and impress any greenhorn by telling them what time it is.

HEIGHT OF ANYTHING
Given that you know how far away you are from an object, you can measure its height. Sight to the top, pinch off the weighted line at the cutting edge of your blade, Then multiply the stepped-off ground distance by the indicated percentage.

Thus you can find:
The height of a tree when you need a certain length pole.
Where a fallen tree top will land.

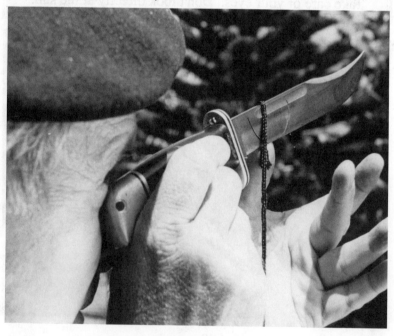

Elevation of an unmapped mountain top.
Height of intended tree house location.
Your precise elevation from map info.
The bullet drop distance down a mountain side.

As we mentioned earlier, this last item is critical if you are working with ropes. When you are dropping down the side of a cliff and discover you have another 40 ft. to go, the old saying, "I am at the end of my rope," has fatal implications.

LINEAR DISTANCE DOWN A MOUNTAIN

From the top of a mountain, the linear distance down the side of that mountain can be valuable, especially to a hunter, because guess-timating those distances is rarely accurate, so you go home hungry. To do this trick, you need to use a UTM map, (Universal Transverse Mercator) because it's contoured with vertical elevation data. Read the straight down distance by counting contour lines from your target's level to yours.

Then, merely aim your knife down toward the target, and read the percentage off the forward quadrant on the left side of your knife. Multiply the vertical elevation distance by that percentage. Convert

> **Horizontal angles play a big part in helping you get around in the woods like a pro. Stick your knife in some wood sideways, and measure off the blade.**

feet to yards or meters for your rifle sights. Precision long-range bullet placement is covered extensively in *THE GREEN BERETS' GUIDE TO OUTDOOR SURVIVAL.*

MEASUREMENT OF ANGLES

Our first innovative outdoor book is all about never getting lost anywhere. Basically, the book teaches you how to bee-line back to any starting point **without using a map** or back-tracking. Even so, maps have several outdoor uses.

Using the protractor plate, (B) on the right side, you can extend any angle measurement with string, and then transfer that angle to a map.

Lots of outdoor persons like to have magnetic azimuths drawn on their maps. Use the protractor plate (B) to remodel your map by transferring the legend's declination data to the map grids. Block off the correct angle on your knife, then move the knife on the map and retrace the angle.

RESECTION

If you can recognize two monuments and identify these on your map, you can find your location. All the other books teach you to use a compass for this and mathematically declinate. A much better way is to use your knife so you don't have to mess around with math.

Stick your knife in a tree or lay it on a flat surface (right side of the blade up) so the knife blade is flat. Now, take sighting shots at the monuments you recognized on your map by stretching strings in their direction.

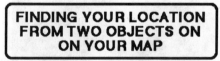

FINDING YOUR LOCATION
FROM TWO OBJECTS ON
ON YOUR MAP

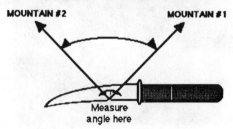

MOUNTAIN #2   MOUNTAIN #1

Measure
angle here

Lay your knife flat on the map and extend those same angled lines to the mapped landmarks.

16

You'll find your location on your map at the place where those two lines cross.

DISTANCE ACROSS WATER OBSTACLES

River crossings can be dangerous. Without any planning, you go into the water and try to swim for it, but the current carries you past your intended landing spot, down to a place in the river where you can't get out of the water. To prevent this, you need to know:

A. Distance from river bank to the other side.

B. Distance to the tie-off anchors for your rope. Is your rope long enough?

C. Speed of the water's current.

D. How fast your designated swimmer swims.

Let's find the river crossing distance. Find an easy landing, a place on the other side where you can get out of the water easily. That's where we will plan to land your cold, water-logged body.

We assume that the river is roughly the same width throughout its course, especially the part that you've elected to swim in. If it isn't or you have any doubts about your swimmer's stamina, add a safety factor to your distance data.

With your knife flat, (stuck in the side of a tree) take two sightings. The first measures across the river to a landing point. The second measures ninety degrees upstream on your side of the river to the end of an isosceles triangle. Once you know where these two places are, mark your position. Perhaps tie a handkerchief on a branch, or hack a blaze mark in the side of a tree.

Now go upstream until you can read 45 degrees to your intended landing spot across the river, and 45 degrees back to the position you just marked. It should look like the following:

SAFE RIVER CROSSING

Measure the current first

45°

b

45°

Side a = Side b

17

Side A = side B because you just made an isosceles triangle, with the triangle's 90 degree angle where you first marked your position (handkerchief or blaze mark).

Step off the distance back to the handkerchief, and that distance will be equal to the distance across the river.

Now, think about the current. You know how fast you swim the distance you just measured. Is the water moving faster? Toss in a floater (piece of wood) and use a stop watch to measure how fast it travels a distance equal to the river's width. If the current is moving faster than you can swim, (maybe twice as fast), go into the water twice as far upstream.

Finally, modify your knife to use as:

A MEASURING TOOL
FOR DEVELOPING A SQUARE ANGLE

Even if your knife's overall measurement is 13 1/8 inches, call that one unit of length, and lay out the sides of a triangle in a ratio of 3, 4 and 5, to create a right angle accurate enough to be used for construction. For any structure in the middle of the wilderness, square corners are important if you want the roof to fit.

Once modified with our clinometers, you and your knife will do a lot better in the woods.

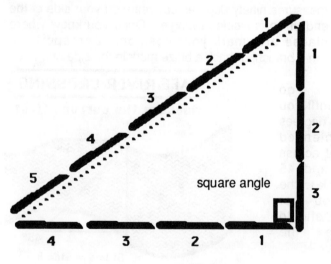

square angle

Chapter 2

MULTI-PURPOSE CONVERSIONS FOR SHEATH AND KNIFE

You could live like an absolute king in the woods if you could take everything with you. But to take it all along, you would need a Mac truck. So the key to better outdoor life is to learn how to use one thing in a variety of ways.

Of course, we'll fix up your knife to do a lot of chores it never did before. Even before we start on your knife, though, let's...

IMPROVE THE SHEATH

I wonder if the people who make sheaths ever think about how you'll be using them. Wouldn't you guess, that with the abundant blessings in brain power God brought into America, somebody would think, "Gee, these things have been the same for a long time now. Maybe we could think of an improvement?" Nope. Sheath makers show me all the innovative imagination of a country cafe owner who names his place, "EAT." Their sheaths hang down straight, flop all over your belt and do almost nothing besides contain the blade—right side up—of course.

That pretty much states the problem. You can be part of the solution. Let's make some make improvements.

19

The sheath on most knives comes with a giant belt loop so your knife hangs loosely on your belt, and changes location often. Don't put up with it. Customize. Think about having your knife hang high on your belt so it doesn't slice rump as you slide into your truck. Move your knife where you want it, and aim it between 15 and 25 degrees forward. Put two beads of leather glue where you want your belt to fit snugly. Once the sheath's loop is tightened to fit, you can reach for your knife confidently because it will stay where you put it. The forward aim will allow you to draw your knife to the rear (quicker and easier) and later, after you add a light, it will shine forward to illuminate your walking path.

ANGLED GLUE LINES FOR KNIFE SHEATH LOOP

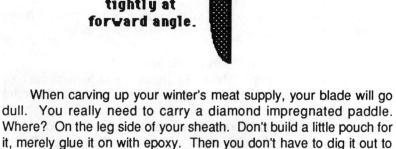

Glue lines for knife sheath so belt slides in to hold knife and light tightly at forward angle.

When carving up your winter's meat supply, your blade will go dull. You really need to carry a diamond impregnated paddle. Where? On the leg side of your sheath. Don't build a little pouch for it, merely glue it on with epoxy. Then you don't have to dig it out to use it, and the sheath can act as a holding paddle.

While you have the glue in your hand, cut the wrist straps off an L.E.D. watch and and attach the time piece to your sheath also. If you get a cheapo high-quality Timex, you can use your watch at night. That's important if you are recording travel vectors so you can bee-line back without a map. Close one eye when noting the time

20

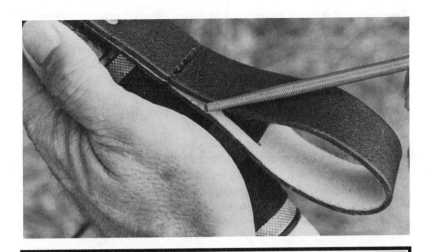

to make sure you preserve your night vision.   Flat-file the back of the watch so it won't catch on your pants. If you are doing a lot of woods-engineering, buy a watch that incorporates a calculator. You can use the storage room you created in your loop to carry a spare battery.

Night travel is necessary in most of the outdoor terrain you will visit. In the desert during the summer, of course, you need to hole up during the day and move at night. In cold weather, you may not have enough gear with you to bed down at night, but you can sleep in the sun during the day. Of course, if you're tactical, you move at night because we have NVG's, (Night Vision Goggles) and the other side's best night trick is an Iraqi match soaked in vaseline. In any of the above cases, you travel

FORWARD LIGHT FROM YOUR KNIFE SHEATH LIGHTS YOUR PATH

Light forward angle at 15°

after dark. Night travel is difficult, though. Snakes are out feeding at night and you can't see trip lines and traps.

Buy a penlight and tape it to the forward part of the sheath. With the sheath tied down to your thigh, you can flip the penlight on and every time you step forward in pitch dark, it will be like The Word in Psalms 119:105—"a lamp unto your feet and a light unto your path."

Anyway, you'll thank God for the light at your feet if you have to carry 200 lbs. of meat out in the woods after night falls.   A fan beam is best for civilian use, but if you're tactical for any reason, tunnel the light. Tape a piece of cardboard around the penlight to contain the light beam. That way, others can't see you walking in the dark.

IMPROVING YOUR KNIVES

In addition to keeping your knife edge sharp, you need to swing it faster for chopping. Speed only helps a little, so add weight to the tip.

> **Why not make use of the back of your sheath? It can sharpen your knife and do outdoor math for you. With a little glue and know-how from this book, you'll become the master of the outdoors.**

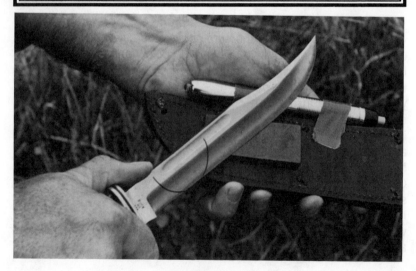

22

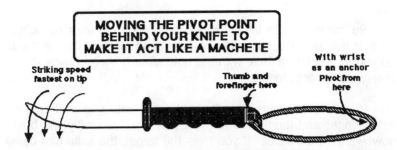

**MOVING THE PIVOT POINT
BEHIND YOUR KNIFE TO
MAKE IT ACT LIKE A MACHETE**

Striking speed
fastest on tip

Thumb and
forefinger here

With wrist
as an anchor
Pivot from
here

First, though, let's pick up the speed. Drill the pommel to receive a thong or lanyard. The thong needs to be just large enough to wrap around the wrist. With the thong snugly attached, you can strike with your knife by holding it loosely and letting the top of your wrist (to the rear of your pommel) act as the pivot point.

The rotation speed stays the same, but you lengthen the radius of the swing so that the velocity on the new, outside arc increases substantially. With such a trick you can convert your knife into a mini-machete, and notch wood a lot faster to make shelter or a weapon in a hurry.

First knife I ever drilled. A lanyard costs nothing, and gave me security when the knife was open. Besides, I could use the lanyard to pry my knife back out of anything. Without one, the best I could do was grip & pull.

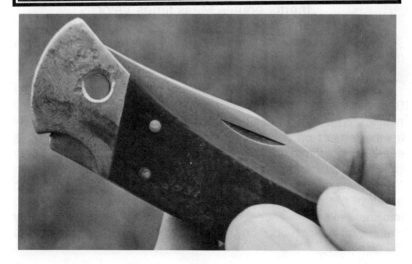

23

Be careful not to let the rough hole edge cut your parachute cord or lanyard. Counter sink the hole, then ream or file the rough edges. If you buy a knife with the hole already there, check to see that its edges are smooth.

In use, let the knife slide forward out of your grip until only the index finger and thumb are left to guide it as you whip the blade downward. Be careful. If you miss the target, the knife can come back at you. Therefore, **make sure not to let blade rotation ever be in line with your body.** Jerry Younkins, (author of *Combat and Survival Knives)* has a much more effective way to cut thick pieces of wood. Set the knife edge on the material and tap the back of the blade. He calls it his, "chisel cutting technique." It's much more effective.

If you're chopping into a tree, you need a heavier blade (like an axe) so that the faster swinging blade sinks into the target. Velocity is desirable, but wood and bone are chopped successfully because of the moment of inertia your blade delivers. You might want to think of inertia as clout; that's why axes are used for chopping; the head of the axe weighs more. If you swing with the same speed, but double the head weight, the blade will bite far deeper in a tree.

Since

$$I = M \times V$$
Inertia equals Mass times Velocity

you get much more penetrating knife strikes by adding weight (Mass) to the front of the blade (the highest velocity area).

Here's how: It's almost impossible to drill a hard blade, (the Buck factory said I might try a laser) so you may have to grind a few notches in the clip. Watch the heat when you do this; let's not screw up the temper on the whole blade. Knives and drunkards have something in common. They both become pretty useless when they blow their cool and lose their temper. If the blade can be ground (use cutting oil) however, you can add clamp-on fishing sinkers with a pair of pliers. Pry the weights apart first by wedging down hard into the sinker with your knife. Another way: Use a small screw clamp with sticky rubber on the faces. Then attach the weights to the clamp.

Adding an ounce of weight at the tip of the knife is the same as adding two ounces halfway back to the pivot point. The increase in weight-leverage gives you added inertia. With an ounce of weight at the tip, plus the change of pivot point to a place behind the knife's pommel, you convert your knife into an axe-like machete, and you can chop a lot thicker branch, or cut down a tree.

Put a hole through the tip of the sheath, and attach a thong. Knife writer Jerry Younkins (he also writes for *Blade Magazine*) likes a thong hole too because it lets water drain out of the sheath. He wrote:

"Water on wood no good.
Water on steel, bad deal."

With the hole through the tip of the sheath, you move the pivot point forward beyond the tip of the knife. Then, with the knife snapped in the sheath, you can thong your wrist again, and pound with the pommel. If your pommel is made of aluminum (Buck), flatten out a spot on the bottom with a file and drill into it. Tap the hole and thread it. A machine screw will then hold the head on— but don't trust the screw alone; use metal glue also. Incidentally, a corrugated head won't slip off a nail as easily, so cross-file that hammer striking surface with a good triangular file.

While you're grinding or filing, take off all the sharp edges on the handle. Your knife is supposed to dig into something other than

You and your file can make most knives friendlier.
Don't let your knife handle cut into your hand.

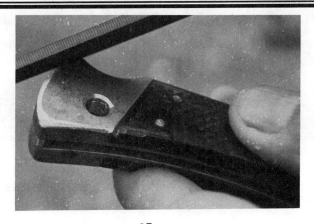

25

your hand. Sure, it costs money to bend metal quillions, and nobody's hand will fit it the same when you do.

But you can fix this problem. What you want is a knife with no rough edges, and nothing on or near the handle that could hurt you if you're using the knife in difficult circumstances. Almost all quillions can be improved by grinding the upper part at a forty-five degree angle so your thumb rests there comfortably.

On some of the old models, (such as Buck's) you need to round off so the hand grip to make it lighter and more comfortable.   So file some of the brass off when rounding it.

MAKE YOUR KNIFE A LIFE-SAVER
Just about every year, somebody gets lost in the woods. But a wife or mother figures out they should have been back so a search

plane is sent. The plane never sees the lost party though, and they die from exposure. If only they had a way to signal the plane!

Put one side of your blade on a buffing wheel. With lots of jeweler's rouge, bring up a shiny surface and convert the concave (blood groove) surface into a signal mirror.

For signal accuracy, cut another groove across the back of the blade with a triangular file. Tape or glue anything flat over the notch to make a sighting hole. First, aim at the sun, then rotate the knife so the hole aims at the target you want to signal. The curved surface inside the blood groove will provide you with a good, long, flash message. If you use your knife for dressing game and you don't want the reflected sun to broadcast your position all over the woods, simply cover the polished area with a piece of tape.

THE ESSENCE OF SAFE COMBAT. INCREASING RANGE.

If you watched our Apache gunships knock out Hussein's Russian T-72 tanks, you saw the principle of Range in action. The helicopters were too far away for the tanks to shoot, and the tanks were well within missile range. Result—Adios, Saddam.

If you fall out of fellowship with a bear or a wild pig in the woods, I recommend that you keep some distance between the two of you—unless you like scars. Bears and boars are like fast-food eateries—-they like to charge before dinner. Don't let them get away with it. You'll enjoy things a lot more if you take the meal out of their hide.

KEEPING AWAY FROM DANGER BY USING RANGE

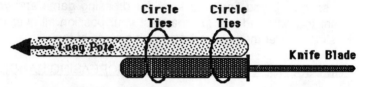

You can get the distance you need by attaching your knife firmly to the end of a long wooden pole. That way, whatever wild animal charges you impales itself and becomes a wild dinner.

File or grind two grooves in a half circle around the side of the handle. Once that's done, use the knife as a jig and line it up by laying it next to a long pole. Put two similar grooves in the pole. After that, you can make a spear in seconds by cinching up a pair of plastic ties over both grooves. Then, you can keep distance between you and danger. Later, if you have time, add security to the tie off with parachute cord.

One of the most popular knives sold today is the S.A.K. (Swiss Army Knife). It's really a handle-full of useful tools. Tune it up; run the grinder over the tip of your phillips-head screw driver so the edges sit down in the screws. Sharpen the blades with a fine stone or diamond and hold ten degress so you have a surgical tool.

Now your knives are versatile. They will cut more—better and quicker. You can change their combat effectiveness by extending range. You will have more control, and they will handle perfectly as you make them do what you want. In short, they will perform better than ever before, which translates to this: You'll become a real pro in the woods.

The rash of handgun sales in San Diego during '91, and the millios a year sold in Miami tell us the country is big on defensive firepower. That's OK, but what about knives? You can't use a pistol to do the work of a knife. But a knife can do a lot of pistol work. In the world of preparation for survival and a great outdoor style of living, knives don't get the attention they deserve.

Chapter 3

HOW TO CHOOSE
THE KINDS OF KNIVES YOU NEED

Choose your knife very carefully if you only plan to carrying only one. To get that one knife to perform well for you, figure out how you'll use it. That's tough. Most good outdoor women and men have many different things to do with a knife. They dress out small game, cook, chop wood, start fires, make traps and shelter and perform minor first aid. Getting one knife to accomplish all those functions is impossible.

But you don't have to carry **just** one. You can carry several. Since knives don't weigh much, even to a backpacker, you can go into the woods or jungle with as many as four knives. If you have to, cut down on weight by eliminating something else, but carry several knives. To make good choices, think about **all** the reasons you need knives, then get every blade you need. Think, for example, about keeping one super-sharp blade in reserve. When you do that, you'll always have a knife ready for field surgery. All things considered, the gain in utility and performance from several knives will make outdoor life more enjoyable and much easier.

Catagory #3: Folders with lockback blades. This is the knife for daily use. They open wih one hand, carry in half the space, and go in a variety of places on your body. Every good woman should own one.

The list of knives you might consider for outdoor, woods use might go something like this:

1. A <u>big blade</u> like a Gurkha Kukri
2. A fixed handle sheath knife to hang off your belt.
3. A folder, probably with a lockback blade.
4. A small pocket knife, perhaps with some tools in the handle, such as a Swiss Army Officer's.

In the city, your knife choice should be different. You don't need big blades for shelter construction. But you might have to repair a car or a mountain bike, or perhaps you need a knife to defend against some of the nastier customers in the neighborhood. So, your list might look like this:

1. A lockback, one-hand opening, folding knife with a blade just under four inches.

2 Either a Swiss Army, a Buck Wenger, or an SOG tool clip.

3. A keychain knife. (My wife uses hers as many as four times a day.)

Some outdoorsmen purchase knives with the wrong motivation. Perhaps:

> This Swiss Army knife allows you to do a variety of chores--anywhere.

A. They liked the knife's looks.
B. They liked the knife's balance.
C. It made them feel macho to carry it.

But the correct criterion for choosing a knife is "D, none of the above."

Suppose you could carry only one knife. To choose the very best knife for you, personally, think about several factors. How will you use it most? Are you tall enough to carry a bigger blade? Can you handle a heavy knife? Would a folder or a sheath knife work best for you?

> Ideal women's knife. Penetrates, then cuts.

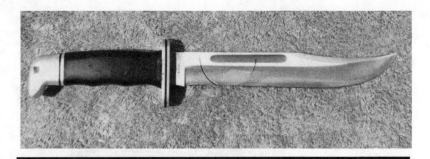

We developed most of our outdoor concepts on this model.
But, a smaller size will do the same tricks, plus be easier to
carry. Make sure knife tip is higher than the back of the blade.

In *Great Livin' in Grubby Times*, we discussed thoroughly how
to choose 'n use a survival weapon. Begin with an accurate
assessment of yourself, followed closely by an assessment of your
needs. Just as you carry a small bore pistol with a big bore rifle, you
can carry a small pocket knife along with your big bowie.

The same applies to choosing your knife. Do you live in a rural
area full of wild animals, or are you surrounded by a concrete jungle
full of wilder animals? Will you use your knife every day or only
infrequently? Are you: Male or female? Strong or weak? Big or
little?

One other factor in knife choice to consider is this: Will you be
using your knives alone or will you most likely partner up with a
friend? Perhaps you're usually with your wife, or, you frequently
hunt or camp with a buddy. A big part of the *Green Beret's Guide to
Outdoor Survival* taught you how to form a survival team
successfully. One reason for forming a team is to utilize the diverse
talents of the team's members. That's what we do in Special
Forces. If you have a variety of talents available to your team, your
chances of winning in conflict or surviving are much greater.

That's also true with knives. As an individual, you probably
need to carry four knives with you, but you still have to consider
carefully how you'll be using them, how big you are, etc. If you're
part of a team, however, you can achieve near perfect skinning,
slicing, trapping, rope-cutting, and demolition ability just by allocating

different knives to different team members. That's one area in which Army Special Forces screws up. Here you get a diversely talented team—-still adhering to the Army's idea of standardizing equipment—-14 men, all carrying the same (double edged dagger?) blade. That's not too bright. Standardization works OK when your ammunition fits your buddy's rifle, but all knives already fit most hands. (We'll show you how to make it do that in another chapter.)

Camillus high country hunters Curved cutting edges for skinning big game. Penetrating point on left.

What you need is a wide variety of sizes and blade shapes.

Therefore: You can really specialize in knife selection for yourself if you know a buddy has a different blade in case you need to do a special job. If you're a team member or you always go into the field with a buddy, choose your blades with that in mind, and do the choosing together so you cover any possible situation.

How will you use your knives? If the primary purpose might be to provide food and you live in the tropics, think about a rust-proof big blade to knock a coconut apart. In the desert, you could be a little more careless about the rust free qualities. In the mountains, you'll find good meat to eat on animals. But, there's a problem; they require skinning. So a skinning blade is a good idea. If you spend much time outdoors, you may learn to trap. A big knife will help you prepare all kinds of wooden gadgets. A small knife is valuable for making trip-line triggers.

ONE OF THE NECESSARY TRICKS A TACTICAL KNIFE MUST PERFORM

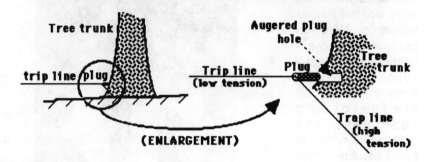

(ENLARGEMENT)

When you have decided what you can work with and what you need, look over what's available. Basically, you have two categories to choose from. Your knife blade either stores in the handle to make a short package, or the handle and blade are fixed, which often requires a carrying place on your body about nine inches long.

Knives with blades folding into the handle:
> Pocket knives
> Folding belt knives
> Clipits.
> Balisong, or, butterfly knives

Knives with blades and handles fixed open.
> Hunting or Sheath Knives
> Survival Knives
> Gurkha Kukri knives

Of course, other kinds of knives perform special tasks better than any of the basic four. Some other kinds include:

Machetes and bolo knives
Throwing knives / shurikens
Stubbies and T-handles
Dive knives/prybars

First, let's look at some knives with blades stored in the handle:

POCKET KNIVES

Arguments against. I have never been much of a pocket knife person. The bulge in my pocket is uncomfortable. The little folding knives fall out of my pants pockets everywhere. More than that, I hate using any knife on which the blade can collapse on my hand. I like my fingers...

Arguments for. First, you can overcome the pocket-carry problem. Buy a black nylon sheath and carry your pocket knife on your belt. After I switched my carry method, I sharpened a two-bladed Buck knife so well once that it performed like a razor blade on the rabbits I butchered. I needed very little stonework to maintain that blade, and over two years, I probably did 500 rabbits with it.

I doubt if I will ever get rid of my Swiss Army Officers knife. Over the years I have carried it in my backpack and used it for just about everything. Mine has tweezers, scissors, can opener, and even a magnifying glass. I've used the leather punch to modify all kinds of belt and foot gear, and recently, in Fiji, I used the bottle opener several times a day.

> One thing wrong on Swiss Army and other folders for some of us in America is the corkscrew. Many of the wine drinkers in our society stay out of the woods and prefer to sleep on concrete at Sixth and Main. Also, glass (broken wine bottles) creates hazards in the woods. More than a few fires have broken out in California when the suns rays, magnified through broken bottles, ignited some dry grass.

What a utility folder could employ better would be a wood auger blade. It would drill a neat little hole in wood to accept a plug, which is one of the most often used trigger systems for traps and snares. If you learn to set traps, wouldn't you like your trigger system to work flawlessly? Start with a neat, round hole. Cut the branch long. Scrape off the bark. Then use the auger to pick out the correct diameter of branch section for a perfect fitting plug.

If you have to carry a knife in one of your pockets, tie it off with a thong on one of your belt loops. Use shock cord or any other elastic cord to stretch out at arm's length so you don't have to untie your knife to use it. Naturally, if the tie-off keeps the knife from departing your body, it will do the same thing for your hand. Slip your wrist through the thong. That's especially important if you're working over water.

NAMES OF FIVE DIFFERENT BLADE SHAPES

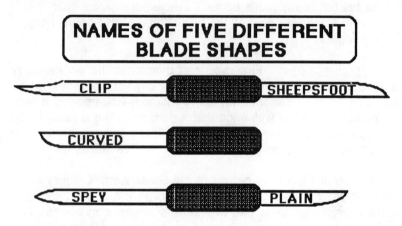

Pocket knives offer five different blades. The beauty of pocket knives is this: Multiple blades broaden your knife's usefulness. One blade does one thing well, while another provides a different, critical function. Probably the best selling pocket knife over the years has been the trapper.

I finally figured out why they called it that. To me, trapping is the art of laying traps and snares for animals and humans. In the old days, however, people used manufactured traps they bought from suppliers. The trapper knife wasn't for making traps; it was for field dressing and skinning the animals caught in those traps.

So the knife featured three folding blades: A clip, a spey, and a sheepsfoot blade. Clip blades can be honed so sharply that the nose is like a needle. Thus, the blade gets under tightly tied parcels and picks splinters out of your hide. The spey blade is the slicer—much like a scalpel. This is a good blade to sharpen to the max, and never use, but know that it's there for field surgery. Of course, it's a great skinning blade for small game if you needed it. Normally, though, that doesn't happen. You can use the clip blade to slice through hide and pull the skin completely off a warm animal. Sheepsfoot blades were originally for trimming sheeps' hooves, but work better today for whittlin' and preparing small wood pieces.

36

Since the end of the blade isn't sharp, you can work your fingers against it safely. By pushing on that rounded end, you can put perfect pressure on the back of the blade and get a precise cut.

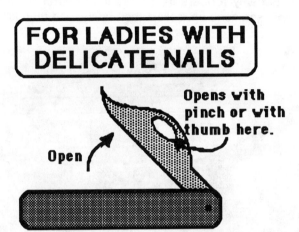

FOR LADIES WITH DELICATE NAILS

Opens with pinch or with thumb here.

Open

Caution. When buying a pocket knife, make sure your finger nail fits the nail nick. What good is a knife if you can't get to the blade? Lots of knives combine too strong a return spring with too small a nail-nick, and it takes a pair of pliers to make the knife usable. **Moreover,** I don't think I could be persuaded to buy a folding knife today that I couldn't open one handed. One-handers today come in two varieties: The hole opener (found on the Clipit line) and the stud openers. Either way, all you have to do is draw your knife and flip the blade to use your knife. That's valuable for working people who have something already in their second hand when they need a knife. If you already own a lockback folder you can't open with one hand, get a U.S. Calvary Catalog, 1-800-333-5102 for $3. In 120 pages of hi-tech outdoor gear, they include a bolt-on stud so you can fix your knife to open with one hand.

Even with a decent, workable nail-nick, the knife is useless for many **women** who have their nails done. The women absolutely need a one-hand opening folder. With one arm load of groceries, she can get the knife ready when she sees what might be trouble in the parking lot. Then if the trouble develops, she's ready to attack by surprise and cut.

On a flight over Louisiana with a sheriff recently, he told me that State was number two in per capita rate of homicide. He couldn't understand why robbers in the French Quarter of New Orleans would hold someone up, collect their booty, and then kill the victim.

Count on <u>Cold Steel</u>. (Write 2128 D Knoll, Ventura, CA 93003.) You don't have to open this knife; it unsnaps from a lightweight, hard nylon sheath. Cold steel pioneers many new and novel designs to fit your needs. This one, a great defender. Under $30!

I know why. It's because the stolen credit cards don't get reported as quickly when the victim dies, and therefore have a higher value with fences. Therefore, this is what your death is worth around the French Quarter of New Orleans: An extra $1,000 or so in credit card fence value.

Even if the knife you already own is only a plain folder with no access for one-handed opening, try to modify it so you can get it open easily with one hand. Your lockback will be a little stiff out of the box. Take a little rubbing compound, mix it with oil, and work it down into the knife joint so your blade works free. Besides that, add some rough tape around the nail nick to improve your grip.

With continued working of the pivot with the lapping compound and a good gripping surface on the blade, you can shake your knife open. Of course, that's second best; if you shake it open you wind up holding the blade rather than the handle, and you still have to transfer to the other hand to achieve your goal. Better that you own a knife on which you can flip the blade open and wind up ready for action with the handle firmly in your hand.

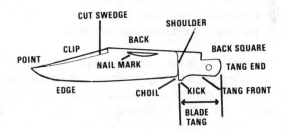

FOLDING BELT KNIVES
If you hunt out of a truck, (example: bear with dogs) you will be getting in and out of your vehicle a lot. Usually, your pistol hangs off one side and your knife hangs on the other, so you end up (pun intended) sitting on one of them.

Folding belt knives are almost as effective as good hunting knives. You can fix your knife so it has a one-hand opening stud and a bolster hole, but the lockback feature on the blade has to come from the factory. Lockback folders carry up, out of the way, and are concealed by most jackets. You won't even know it's there unless you reach for it. Of course, folders are not the knife of choice to use for cooking; food particles stuck to the blade work their way into the handle crevice and will create a high bacteria count on the blade's cutting edge.

Several companies make folders with more than one blade, so you get a variety of good uses out of the same handle. Remington's Big Game knife provides a lock-back for both blades. One clip blade penetrates and skins (somewhat), and the other has a gut hook on the end of a boning saw. Gut hooks are miserable to sharpen, and you shouldn't need to cut through bone in the field. Animals were designed by God to come apart at the joints when tendons are cut.

If you're thinking of buying a folding knife and it doesn't have the blade lock-out feature, forget it. It's only an overgrown pocket knife in a belt pouch, and when the blade collapses on your hand, you'll bloody wish you'd bought the real thing.

One hunting season in Oregon, a folding knife was all I used. I dressed out a couple of deer and a bear with it. The knife was a little short for the tasks, but it was a dream to carry.

A marlinspike knife is for yachtsmen or fishermen. You use the spike for splicing rope and taking out knots that would never respond to finger picking. For hunters and outdoorsmen, however, ropes are being replaced with other fasteners, (see Shelter in Book II of *Everybody's Outdoor Survival Guide*) so the marlinspike knife may lose some popularity.

FIXED BLADE KNIVES. COMBAT.
In my opinion, noone should buy a combat knife without buying a training knife made of rubber. If you own one and don't practice with it, you're just asking for trouble when you try and make it work for you. Path Finder's philosophy on combat, however, is **don't.** Knives get you into criminal trouble if you win because you assulted a lesser-armed villain with a deadly weapon. If you go up against an opponent with a firearm, you just give him an excuse to pull the trigger. Finally, in a tie, both parties to the conflict lose. Therefore, your chances are lose, lose, or go to jail. Bigger blades are better because they give you more reach. Therefore, you can extend your range from your opponent and move in when you have an opening. Consider, for example, the Mamba from Black Jack Knives. Cold Steel makes the TrailMaster, which is a long bowie-type blade. Tanto, also from Cold Steel is a good combat knife because the tip of the blade angles back so it slices nicely.

From Chris Peiffer collection

You need to carry a second compass, and hollow handle knives are a great choice for survival. Note holes in quillion and screwdriver

HUNTING KNIVES

If you understand the difference between a sports car and a four wheel drive truck, you can understand the difference between a folding belt knife and a hunting knife. The little folder will get you in and out of some tight spots, and it will park easily in a smaller pouch, but the big guy has power and can cut quite a load. Of course, big knives can't squeeze into tight places, and they require a big parking spot on your body.

When we say "hunting knife" we're talking about solid, strong handled, sheathed, non-folding, hunting knives. People call them belt knives because that's the way they are most often carried. Almost all come with a quillion (hand guard that keeps you from slicing your fingers off on a forward plunge).

Some of the features to look for: Kraton handle, pommel hole, with sleeve. Serrated cutting edge near quillion, and non-slip thumb rest. Penetrating point on clip shape.

Hot rodders say, "if it doesn't go, chrome it." We feel the same way about knives. "If it won't hold an edge, adorn and engrave it." To us, knives are a tool, and drawing fancy pictures on them doesn't make a lot of sense.

Before folding belt knives came along, a hunting knife was your main cutter. Most big game hunters still prefer them because they do a big job quickly. Anybody who hunts a lot really needs one, because pocket knives are just a little too flimsy for dressing big game. Others will choose the big blade because they chop limbs, make traps and weapons or work as a quick step when driven into a tree. Since the big hunting knife is not going to be your one and only, I recommend it. The bigger the better.

The knife you choose 'n use often depends on how much time you have to field dress the game you bag. The time factor is most critical to a hunter at the end of the day. Here's the problem: You hunt all day when most big game is bedded down. Deer, for example, drop down during the day with a view downwind, then let their nose warn them of approaching man from upwind. This way, they stay somewhat safe. About an hour or so before sundown, they move around to feed. That's when most meet "deer Maker."

Once your game is bagged, your major military mission is to get your meat out of the woods before nightfall. You'll have to cover the distance to your camp or truck in daylight if you have any respect for your shins. If you have to carry it out of the woods in the dark, stumbling will make the meat on your lower legs look something like the animal you just butchered. Also, you'll get lost easier at night (unless you have our *Compass Course Book*). Thus, many outdoorsmen try to go faster. But it's hard to save time by bookin' thru the woods with over a hundred pound load on your back. Also, it's physically risky; if you twist an ankle, count either on staying out a few extra days, or using your knees for feet.

So, here's the situation report: Aim your knife at the top of the sun quickly and read the daylight left on your clinometer. You have only a certain time to get out of the woods if you want to complete that travel in daylight, plus you'll need time to field dress your groceries.

42

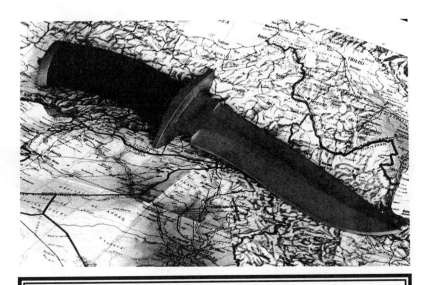

Operation Desert Storm Knife by Bardsley has some great features. Top of knife is straight, and quillion could be drilled for sighting. Thicker spine to the point gives strength for prying. Curved cutting edge helps make this blade a good slicer.

In Oregon, I hunted bear with Jim Minter and his pack of hounds. A bear does all right with hounds as long as he runs downhill. Uphill, however, the dogs use developed hind quarters to close in. Result, the bear usually trees a long way down and a few hundred yards up. By the time I usually arrived at the tree, I'd be spent.

One bear I shot departed this world an hour and a half before sundown. I knew where I was exactly; it would take me an hour and a quarter to get to the main road. My knife told me I only had an hour and a half left before it got dark. It doesn't take an Inspector Clouseau to figure out I only had fifteen minutes to dress that carcass out. Fail to make my dress-out deadline and I would probably dress out my shins in the dark.

That's what happened. Though I didn't need to skin an inch on that bear because the hide and head would go to the taxidermist, all I had with me was a raised point skinning knife. So it took me over a half hour before I could leave. That meant I'd be late, and I would be carrying in the dark. Since I had just hustled 1,700 ft. downhill, then 300 feet back up another hill, I was puppy-dog tired. My shins still bear witness to my poor timing. Scars.

The whole story makes this point: when daylight is fading, you need a knife you can work with—-fast and efficiently. Drop point or falling point blades open an animal quickly so you lighten the carry without tainting any meat. Also, you need a hefty blade to cut

Saw teeth on the back of a blade often weaken it. Here, the blade is long enough to make teeth effective. Clip-shaped point makes this knife a good pole spear attachment. Hollow handle carries survival goodies. Great thong attachment. Handle wrapped in cord provides utility in the field. Any mother wearing combat boots should be proud to own one.

through hind quarter joints in case you divide the weight or need to make two trips. If the folding belt hunter you carry doesn't do everything you require, carry a bigger blade to put horsepower into your butcher work.

What really do you need in the field? As we taught in *Everybody's Outdoor Survival Guide*, you really need to know how to make a fire. That means chop wood—either by saw or axe.

So—-knife makers frequently cut a saw edge on the back of their big knives. But, that's not the best idea. Our book dealers in Alaska tell us that saw tooth knives often break. Where? At a tooth cut. Chop through whatever you need in half; it's faster and easier. I had lunch recently with Jerry Younkins, a prominent knife writer. Rest assured, he does his homework. He tells me you can tap on the back of a blade and thus drive it into a limb as you roll around the sides and press in ever deeper with each tap. It works great and

you would be surprised at the size of some limbs he has cut with only a small blade! We designed the PAKA (in this book) with a pivoting handle so you can chop things easily. That's also why we figured out how to move the pivot point behind the knife pommel with a lanyard, and thus chop with more force. Finally, the chopping function is the reason we settled on the Kukri as such a great addition to your regular field knife complement.

FISH AND FILLET IT.

To work on fish best, you need more than one knife blade. You need to take off the scales. You need to cut through the skin (use a box knife, especially on tuna), and you need to cut thin slabs of meat off the bone.

Bigger knives are simply too unwieldy for fish. Use a fillet blade, which is a long, slender, flexible blade with a sharp, fine point and an upswept tip. This last feature gives the knife a sweeping curve so that it fillets with a flip of the wrist while the blade is deep into the meat.

Any fishing or boat knife needs to float. When your hands are full of slime on a rocking boat, your knife has a good chance of slipping out of your hand. If it sinks, wave good-bye. Some knife-makers still confuse their knives with fishing tackle. When a knife hits the water, it shouldn't turn into a sinker. If you bought one of these, drill a hole in the pommel and tie a float on it so you can get it back out of the drink if it slips.

You'll be a lot safer with your knife if its handle has a good grip. I recommend Kraton, that sticky rubber first used by Cold Steel. If your knife handle is some chintzy, small hard black plastic, size it first by adding plastic wood or wrapping the handle—-preferably with parachute cord you can use in an emergency.

45

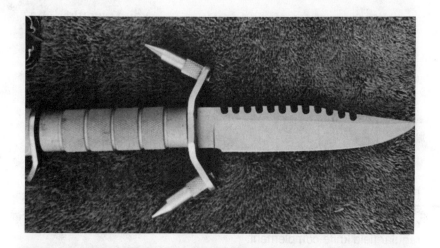

Spikes in the quillion at an angle would allow you to use your knife as a grappling hook. Lanyard attachment is solid. A hollow handle is great storage, but normally, the stuff inside is junk. Write to MPI to get a can of replacements.

Or, buy a bicycle inner tube. Coat the inside with slippery rubber cement, and slide a cut section of the tube over your handle so you have a good gripping surface. The bike tube rubber will also insulate your hand from temperature extremes or electrical current you might feel by touching the tang.

You can purchase either a fixed-blade sheath fillet knife, or a folder. I prefer the former with a long blade, but I wouldn't hesitate to own a folder if carrying it around a boat was important. Make sure the blade is stainless, especially if fishing in salt water. Also, pick a blade that has been heat treated so it's <u>hard</u>. With today's diamond sharpeners, you can put an edge on a lot easier, so edge durability is more important than a soft, easy-to-sharpen cutting edge.

SURVIVAL KNIVES
Ever since the movie, *FIRST BLOOD,* a new breed of knives for survival has sold well. I give Rambo credit; (Stallone got two copies of our *Everybody's Outdoor Survival Guide* in Hawaii.) *First Blood* gave birth to many survival knives, including our own design, the PAKA.

One more good use for a big blade. When you hold the blade behind your back, you can swing out and cut. From that same position, you can upper-arm block an incoming blow from a club. Just make sure to hold the blade flat along your forearm.

Several companies have tried to make a good survival knife and failed. One area in which they come up short is the saw-toothed back. Without tooth-set, the blade will bind in the wood. The dealer at Alaska's Bullet and Blade shop in Anchorage tells me this: "Up here in the cold, steel is put to the ultimate test. If a company's quality control slips, the blades fail, most often when you need reliability the most." He then went on to say that the blades failed most by breaking—right where the tooth cuts were because tooth cuts weaken blade metal.

Still, you may want to buy a survival knife. If you follow our modifications, you can improve the one you buy. Then carry a second pocket knife or folder. But you MUST start with something decent. Pay attention to our chapter on blades. Since a survival knife stays packed and unused for long periods of time, it's a good idea to get a blade that won't rust.

When I first published this book, (440 C) stainless was hot. Even though it was difficult to sharpen, it could hold an edge for a long time. One problem---it was too brittle. Under side stress, it would break. Another small problem, it was so hard that it would dig a small dish into a rough stone so you couldn't use the stone to put a reliable straight edge on your knife anymore.

Now, however, we have better steels and better steel blends. In the early 80's, specialty knives hadn't yet come into popularity the way they have today. In the trade, specialty refers to knives which were designed for a special purpose. The term has a borader meaning today, however; it means knives made with special steel and (sometimes) special plating which will do a great variety of chores---plus stand up under the toughest of tests. Blackjack knives is just one of the firms which make such knives. They use a rather new steel blend which will stay sharp for a long time, but yet isn't so brittle that it breaks.

Don't go for plain, high carbon steel, which will rust and thus fail to cut for you when you need it most. Carbon steel rusts. With a microscope, you could discover just as much pitting along the cutting edge as you would on the side of the blade. Therefore, after long periods of storage, the edge-pited blade couldn't cut. There is only one thing worse than going afield and forgetting something: that's remembering everything, but finding out that what you brought won't cut it.

Probably the new, specialty knives are the most reliable you can own today. They choose their steels most carefully, and then plate or treat that steel so their knives out perform and out last other commercial knives by a wide margin. Even though they cost from 15% to 40% more, the investment is excellent when you consider a return of more than 100% increased performance and reliability.

Blackjack makes a knife so well that Jerry Younkins built a cabin with one. The company tells me they will sharpen any of their knives for free for life, and also will replace any that break. For an extra 15%-40% in cost, that's not bad. Cold Steel's knives are also top of the line, and they'll do just about anything. Take knives from both of these manufacturers out of the box and the edge will shave your arm.

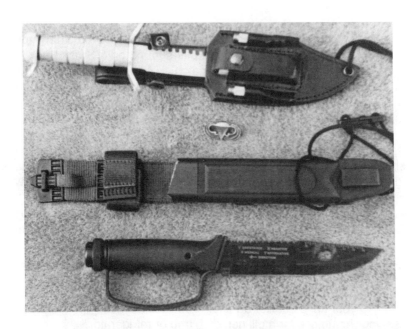

Two decent survival knives. Top has angles quillion for grappling hook spikes, stuffed into sheath. Bottom: The Brewer, designed by Spanish explorer. This guy had his act together, designed knife with hole in tip of blade. Very useful.

If you often play or work around water, make sure your survival knife comes with a rubber O-ring to keep water out of the hollow handle. Almost all are packed with wrong stuff, so **change the goodies in the handle**. The quick and easy way is to buy a survival can from MPI, 37 East St., Winchester, Mass. 01890-1198. The kit has just about everything you'll need—-as specified by the company's design expert.

We've seen some survival knife handles packed with useless junk. Make sure the wire saw works, then lube it really well (Rig/grease) and rewrap it. Cut down on the number of fish hooks to about three. Include at least one barb-less hook so you can sew up a human injury. Add some monofilament fish line. In most survival knives, you can wrap the line around the plastic insert (goodie container), which also helps to cut down on the movement (and noise) inside the handle.

Add wood matches dipped in paraffin. If you cut them too short, you can always use a pair of pliers found on a Swiss Buck to extend your reach with a burning match. Add a twelve foot length of good black nylon thread. Think about a few halizone tablets for purifying water. Use those if you don't have a modern filtration straw to purify water absolutely, even from Giardia parasites.

Some goodie kits contain a scalpel; that's OK if you don't sharpen your smaller blades often. At least you'll have a fresh blade for surgery in the field to cut a snakebite wound open. Add a few butterfly sutures. Then you won't have to push a fish hook through your leg, and any field wound can stay open somewhat, which helps it drain in case the original wound was messy. Finally, add a couple of sewing needles and thread so you can extract splinters or repair your shirt.

Any more room? Add clamp-on fish sinkers for the blade's clip to make your knife act like an axe. You also will need sinkers if you use your hammock for a gill net, crab trap or refrigerator.

The compass has to be small to fit the inside the handle. In order to make it more accurate, enlarge the sight base. Use your blade on a tree stump to sight on a direction in which you intend to move. Push the blade into the wood, and then line your compass up with the cut in the woood.

Make sure your knife has a thong hole. Before you wrap your handle in tape, buy and add two tight fitting key rings to fit over the handle. They make excellent snares when attached to wire.

Wrap part of the handle in shiny fluorescent hot pink tape if you're tactical. Cut a 1/2" piece of that tape off and stick it on the back of your shirt collars. That way, you and your buddy can see each other, but nobody else can.

Don't buy a survival knife without a quillion. Keeping your hand away from the blade is a good idea, and you need something to sight through for accurate woods measurement.

Finally, stone the back edge of the tip as well as the cutting edge. You'll want your knife to cut in two directions—-sometimes to cut through blood vessels in an animal or perhaps in self defense. With a sharp edge on each side of the blade, you can cut foreward or backward with it by flipping your knife back and forth. Also, you want the point sharp so you get easy penetration when spearing. Remember, on a knife with an upswept tip, you can't sharpen the inside-out curve on the back of the blade unless you use a rod, either ceramic or diamond.

A great bolo knife, called "El Cheapo." Claim to fame: Rusts faster than a junk car. Wooden handle by beachbums. Size 22 thong hole by Miss Fire. Marvelous class Z cutting edge by Miss File. But it cuts bananas. . .

THE BIGGIES—FROM BOLO TO BOWIE

Both my Cold Steel Bowie (TrailMaster) and my Black Jack Mamba are big knives. The blades measure 9 1/2 inches. The rule for sheath knife blades is generally: **the bigger the better**. Just make sure you can carry the knife in a way which allows you to use it easily. Several companies now produce big blades with a special sheath. The knife hangs up side down on a pair of suspenders.

If your big blade comes with a belt loop sheath, you can partially solve the in-and-out of a truck problem when you modify the sheath to hang forward. Also, punch a hole in the bottom of the sheath and attach a leather or nylon thong through it so you can tie the knife off on your leg.

Named by *Blade Magazine*, "Best Cutlery Buy of the Year" 1987. Too good a deal, so I bought one.

Blackjack mamba's little brother is a lock back folder. The stud on the blade gives me more positive one-hand opening than a thumb hole. Also, release in center of handle helps prevent accidental lock release by squeeze in heavy use.

By my definition, any blade longer than the nine inches is a biggie. Big blades will do wonders when it comes to slicing and self defense. Blackjack's Mamba is such a blade. Perhaps it's the best, most durably edged and most reliable big knife you can own.

You may encounter the need for a long reach with a big blade you don't have. If that happens, you can make one quickly with the plastic tie system. Even if your extension stick is only a few feet long, you can develop tremendous knife power with a two handed hold and a baseball type swing. Of course, a better way to go with long stick weapons is to use them as a jabbing tool. That way, you get in to the target without sending advance warnings, and you don't risk breaking the pole as much.

If you regularly need a blade longer than 10 inches, you should think about buying a machete. Just about any surplus store will sell one for under $10. They come short (16") or long (24"). Blackjack makes a specialty machete which costs substantially more, but it's worth it. The blade is tapered all the way to the tip. Result: you can swing the thing all day long without getting as tired; also, a lighter tip gives you a lot more velocity, so you fly through jungle brush easier.

BOLO KNIVES wind up somewhere between machetes and bowies for size. The round nose on the top of the blade quickly digs the meat out of coconuts—-my most dependable South Seas food. But while bolo knives are cheap, they don't hold an edge and they rust like Hawaiian junk yard iron. Therefore, you have to work on the edge every time you use them. What's your time worth?

THE KUKRI—-IN A CLASS BY ITSELF

The big deal with this knife is the blade and its utility. Because the tip of the blade is heavy, it chops like an axe. Since the curvature of the sharpened bottom edge is perfect—-far better than an axe—-it chops better. The balance is much better than that found on a camp axe, and you can use this knife for a variety of purposes, including skinning, draw knifing, hasty shelter fabrication, and a host of others.

Similar designs to the Kukri show up from many different factories under a variety of names. This blade is the big one to own if you will go into the field with four knives. Because of the curvature of the blade, it slashes with tremendous cutting power. The angle down from the blade line on the handle allows you to reverse thrust into a target effectively. These knives are better balanced than an axe, and therefore are more controllable. I own a Becker Machax--- it was simply my choice. Black Jack produces Kukri-like blades in a variety of shapes, but the Becker Machax is the best for me because it will do a variety of tasks.

EXTRAORDINARY KNIVES

I'm not very big on T-handled, or push-blade knives. One such contraption is worn like a belt buckle, so you get the element of surprise in attack. Big deal. You work your way in close, and then pull the knife and while you are doing that, you could easily suffer some damage. If you draw before you move in close, your assailant sees the knife, so he knows about your new, offensive capability. If he carries a handgun, your error is probably going to be fatal.

Many manufacturers produce blades under two inches. I can recommend them for keychain carries in the city, and for women. Short knives often become survival knives, however, because that's all you have when a situation arises. Therefore---**don't buy a cheap, short-bladed knife. Spend the extra ten dollars; you'll**

absolutely need the quality when the chips are down. If there were ever a time when quality counted, it would be when you needed a knife in a surprise situation.

Throwing knives sell well after a hit movie uses that action in a stunt. Don't go for it. You can buy throwing knives cheap, and literally destroy some nice tree while learning to be bad, but you shouldn't waste the time.

Butterfly knives take too long to open unless you happen to be a taxi driver in the Phillipines and have time to practice. Most butterfly blades are a bear to sharpen. I defy you ever to sharpen any butterfly knife like the **razor cutters from SpyderCo, Cold Steel, or Blackjack.** Cold Steel makes excellent small knives for defense purposes, and since they are <u>one piece in a nylon sheath,</u> you don't need to open them.

Switch blades and push blades are likewise poor investments. With a one-hand opening lockback blade, you don't have to worry about the blade breaking, and its edge will be far sharper than you anything you can ever hope to develop. Other ways to get double edged cutting and defense utility are with boot knives and daggers, both a bit unwieldy because of the fixed handle. The overall length of the knife will be a bit much to carry.

SPECIAL KNIVES FOR THE CAMP KITCHEN

If you live in the woods, you will be storing and freezing a lot of game—-birds, fish, venison and bear—-perhaps even elk. A good rural house should have two kitchens: one for cooking, and the other for harvesting. Do the same in camp. You need an area for harvesting and one for cooking.

Probably the best idea for any outdoorsperson's kitchen is to stock it with the same four blades you'll carry with you in the woods. A Becker Machax beats a meat cleaver any day. A nine inch blade cuts meat, bread and all kinds of vegetables. A few smaller hunting knives and a fillet knife round out your collection. With these tools in the kitchen, you increase you knife handling and cutting skills daily. Also, those blades will hold an edge far better than most commercial grade kitchen knives. Any magnet tool strip will hold them on a wall. With just one set of knives for both kitchen and field, you can go anywhere and feel right at home.

Why bother to sharpen your knives? Dull knives will cut; you simply have to push and slice harder to make them do their work. That's why dull knives are dangerous. Since wood and animal hide is tougher than your own hide, a slip with a dull knife often means a spill of your own blood. Even so, you may be too busy to keep your blades sharp. That's OK. **Suture self!**

Chapter 4

HOW TO KEEP
THE CUTTING EDGE MAINTAINED

You want to know what it must feel like to play God? Sharpen your blade to the max and slice through a hunk of meat. Watch the two sides fall apart. I bet that's how God felt when he parted the Red Sea for Moses.

To have things fall apart easily when you touch them with your blade takes a little bit of know-how and a few tools. Sharpening devices are like car insurance. Some people spend their last dime to buy the very best car they can afford, and then have no money to spare for insurance. Likewise, you can spend a fortune on the best knife made. Eventually the blade will go dull. If bought a knife the maker won't sharpen for free, or you don't have the money to buy good sharpening tools, your expensive, dull knife will become a liability.

Buy a cheaper knife if you have to, but own the best sharpening tools you can get—and learn how to use them. The cheapest knife with a sharp edge is far better than the most expensive dull blade in the world. Moreover, you can own a great second hand knife for next to nothing if you can find one with a damaged blade and restore it. When you learn to sharpen all your knives and cutting edges to perfection, you acquire one of the great skills of an outdoors master. Kitchen master, too.

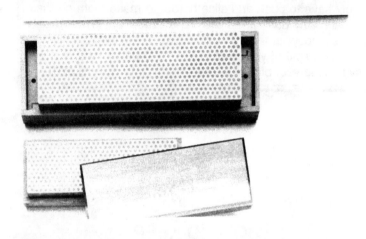

Diamond Machine Technology produces lightweight plastic whetstones made from clumps of diamond abrasives. You need diamond sharpeners for modern steels---unless you have patience beyond Biblical limits. Light pressure = fine edge.

How big should your sharpener be? At least two thirds as long as your biggest blade. So, if you carry a 9" bowie get at least a 6" whetstone. Small stones increase the chance of injury, as do stones you have to hold in two fingers. Sooner or later, you'll get a small stone messy when your thumb or finger bleeds on it. Large stones cost $78, and Diafolds (light enough to carry in a backpack easily) cost only $23.   With coarse (blue color) Diafolds, and you can put a good cutting edge on just about any knife.   They also make a fine grit (red color) for putting on a finer edge. If you own a specialty blade, (Black Jack) stropping is just about all you need.

With only one Diafold, you can put a great edge on a blade; simply use light pressure. Always stroke so the cutting edge leads, never vary the angle, and finish with light pressure to leave a nice cutting edge on your blade.

Carry a Diafold with you in the field; they're lightweight and fairly sturdy. If you need to press down hard because you want to reshape your edge, support the far end of the flat sharpener or round rod at the far end. **Don't** support anything on your knee; there's a good chance the paddle or rod will slip and you'll get an involuntary blood sample out of your leg.

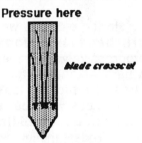

PRESSURE FUNNEL FROM BACK EDGE TO CUTTING EDGE

Pressure here

blade crosscut

Narrows to force here

When you cut anything, all the pressure on the back of the blade is applied to the meat at the narrow cutting edge. When your knife's two side surfaces narrow down to the narrowest, straight cutting edge and run consistently from the point to the back of the blade, we call that sharp. Your blade cuts sharply because the applied knife pressure on the back of the blade is funnelled to the smallest, thin line possible. If you want to think of it as hydraulics, all the pressure on the quarter inch back of the blade is squirting out the tiniest razor-thin line you can create.

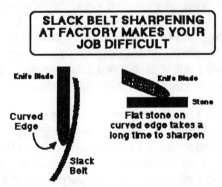

SLACK BELT SHARPENING AT FACTORY MAKES YOUR JOB DIFFICULT

Knife Blade

Curved Edge

Slack Belt

Knife Blade

Stone

Flat stone on curved edge takes a long time to sharpen

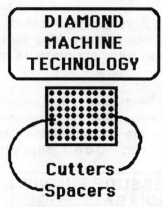

DIAMOND MACHINE TECHNOLOGY

Cutters

Spacers

Your blade came out of the box with one of three grinds: either hollow, slack belt or flat. The first two kinds mean nothing to you because almost all of us resharpen with a flat device. Either diamond block whetstones, rods or Diafold flats do the job efficiently. Spaces between the cutters provide a place for metal filings to accumulate so you always have cutters exposes to your blade.

In the old days we used stones. We started with a rough grit because it took more metal off quicker. Then, progressively, we repeated the process until we finished with a hard Arkansas stone and, (for a super fine edge) a strop. The whole process took a lot of time and required patience. It was tedious work because a sharp job always calls for **one, continuous, thin line on the sharpened edge** of your knife. Today, though, we produce tougher blades. Stones don't work well on these because they dish out, which means you'll never get a consistent edge.

Diamond impregnated sharpeners not only stay flat; they remove metal much faster. Diamond Machine Technology impregnates their devices (both flat and tubular) with millions of diamond crystals in pods. The result: You take metal off about 40% faster. That's important because most knife makers use a slack belt to shape their blades' edges. Therefore, when your knife eventually dulls, you have to take away all that curved surface with a flat diamond whetstone before you do the edge any good.

Translated into knife benefit, DMT (Diamond Machine Technology) sharpeners mean this: a. It takes a lot less time to produce a sharp edge. b. Since the metal comes off the knife a lot easier, you can concentrate better on holding the same angle between the sharpener and the knife edge, which insures that you get one long, finely narrowed, razor edge.

But for so many of us, it just doesn't come out that way. We grind and grind, and never seem to achieve a great edge. Hopefully, this chapter will change that forever. Let's start by asking, "What goes wrong?"

First, we don't hold the knife against the stone at a consistent angle. The back of the blade drops and raises as we zing the knife edge across the abrasive surface. When you change the angle as you move the knife and stone, you create a series of parallel lines running the length of the blade. The resulting edge cuts as if the fine edge were twice or even three times as thick—which is rather dull.

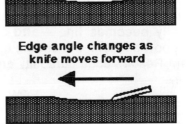

Edge angle changes as knife moves forward

Your stone may dish-out so small you can't see it.

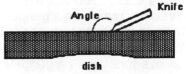

Second, even if we succeed in holding the edge constant, we leave a wire on the edge. Though the knife feels sharp, that wire, or a piece of it, breaks off and takes some edge metal with it. When that happens, the knife edge is dull again.

Even if you had enough patience to use a stone on an old carbon steel blade, the new steels will test that patience to its limit. In fact, sharpening 440 C stainless or ATS-34 steel will test the patience of Job. Believe me when I tell you--- the new steels are a lot tougher; therefore, the knife edge doesn't give way. That means you have to attack them with a tool that will abrade (cut away metal) on the sides of your edge. Only diamonds will do the job quickly.

Start with coarse; finish with fine. Coarse abrasive surfaces leave lots of metal fragments on the knife edge. Thus, the blade tears meat as it cuts. But during use, the blade's cutting edge loses most of those rough little edges, and, as they fall away, the remaining knife edge is thick and dull. That's why we finish the sharpening process on a fine or hard surface; the rough edges are smoothed down until that fine line really becomes fine—-**and** continuous. Then, you get side support all along the cutting edge so fewer rough particles fall off. Result: edge durability and fine, quick cutting.

HOW TO SHARPEN

Begin the sharpening process on any new blade by shaping it up on a coarse (blue) diamond stone. Give priority to a broken tip or a nicked edge. Just take away all the metal around it until you have a smooth, continuous line on your cutting edge. You can use a file (if your knife is soft enough). Just **be careful** on a grinding wheel not to overheat the blade. Once it loses its temper, (hardness), the knife is ruined. You're far better off to remove knife metal by hand than to risk overheating on a grinding wheel. DMT's extra coarse grit will remove metal unbelievably fast.

Make a decision. How much angle do you want on the sides of the cutting edge? Narrow down the edge's angle to about 10 degrees to create a fine cutting edge. That slender metal edge will dull more easily, (on less expensive knives) but the cutting will be wonderful. Ten degrees is fine for small blades and scalpels. For example, put ten degrees on the round edged blade of your trapper pocket knife, then don't use the blade until you have a need for a fine cutter (field surgery).

But, with bigger blades, you can widen the angle. Big blades cut thick objects and often wind up chopping wood. If you angle those edges at 25 -40 , the edge will have more back-up metal behind it, and therefore stand up against more abuse. Basically, the narrower the edge, the more delicate the blade's edge because of less backup metal to reinforce and hold it together.

At the risk of repetition, make sure to keep your angle consistent. It must be the same with every stroke, or you will

60

create two center lines on the cutting edge. Result: You won't cut much more than cheese, and you can do that without a knife.

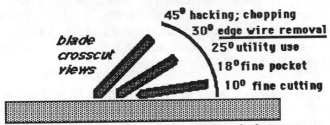

CUTTING ANGLES FOR VARIOUS USES

blade crosscut views

45° hacking; chopping
30° edge wire removal
25° utility use
18° fine pocket
10° fine cutting

side view, diamond sharpener

One way to avoid a broken line along the cutting edge is to use a pair of ceramic sharpening rods. These sticks protrude from a holding block at about 20 degree angles, so all you have to do is run your knife down alternate rods while holding the blade vertical. Rods like these are excellent for sharpening a blade with an upswept edge such as you find on a sheath knife's skinning edge or a spey blade on a folder.

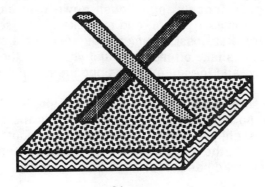

CERAMIC SHARPENING STICKS

Ceramics mounted on a board at a predetermined angle are not the only way to keep the proper edge on your blade. Use our clinometer. Make an enlarged photocopy and cut out the correct angle. Then use a stack of coins as a guide. Rest the back edge of the knife on that stack and hold that angle firmly as you move the knife along.

Better yet, go commercial; you can take the guess work out of sharpening with an adjustable knife jig. DMT makes the angler; I like that best (diamond abrasives). Lansky also makes a similar jig for holding a stone at a consistent angle against the side of your knife edge.

If you sharpen a variety of blade shapes on a flat sharpener, you know how difficult it is to get a sharp edge on some of the curved surfaces. To do that trick with a flat sharpening surface requires that we lift the handle just right, and few of us do it correctly. Thus, the part of the knife we use most has several thin lines of edge metal on it, which make it act like a dull knife.

DMT's diamond impregnated rod will sharpen any cutting edge curve and make it easier to sharpen the curved upswept surface of a blade. Hold the rod steady. Hold the diafold plastic handle vertically and the rod won't flex as much. Also, rest the edge of the rod on the edge of a table. Then hold the knife firmly as you slide it along the rod diagonally so the rod attacks the sides of the **complete** cutting edge. <u>Always slide the knife with the cutting edge leading.</u>

Hold the knife edge against the abrasive metal remover firmly at your chosen angle, push down with clout (elbow grease and shoulder polish), and stroooke . . . Use as long a diagonal stroke as possible, unless you are using a small stone. Smaller devices take off more metal if you move the stone one circular way, and the knife in the opposite circular way.

Make sure to push edge-first into the stroke. Moving the sharpener the other way—edge trailing—curls the edge of the blade over slightly to create the wire we talk about. When the wire breaks off, the thick metal left on the edge won't cut, and we think the knife has a poor edge-holding ability.

To make sure your bench diamond block or stone doesn't move when you push hard against it, secure it to a work bench with cleats, either clamped or nailed. While you're at it, drive a wedge under one end of the stone so that it's natural for you to hold the correct angle when you stroke your blade.

HOME MADE HOLDING BLOCK FOR BIG STONE OR DIAMOND

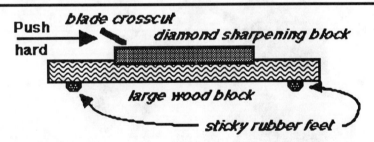

On stones and other cutters without some free space between abrasive, you will notice dark microscopic metal chips gathering on the surface as soon as you start sharpening. So you wind up rubbing metal (knife edge) against metal (grit). Result: you accomplish zip. When that happens, you'll feel the knife sliding smoothly over the stone's surface, rather than grinding. Don't let this happen.

If you're working with tools from the stone age (pun intended) use a good honing oil to float the metal pieces above the stone's surface. By so doing, you ensure that the stone is making solid contact with the blade, and is cutting with the whole contact surface. When the oil on your stone changes to a dark color, wipe it all away with a soft cloth; then reoil it. If you don't remove the chips, the stone can't do its cutting job properly, and progress grinds slowly to a halt. That's one reason I switched to diamond sharpeners. I didn't want to carry a can of (leaky) oil in my backpack. Another reason for diamond sharpeners is ease of cleaning. You can swish the things off in water and they'll be perfectly clean to continue grinding. Also, DMT's flat sharpeners use pods so that the diamond abrasive pods don't fill up with chips. Only the abrasives cut; the spaces collect the grit.

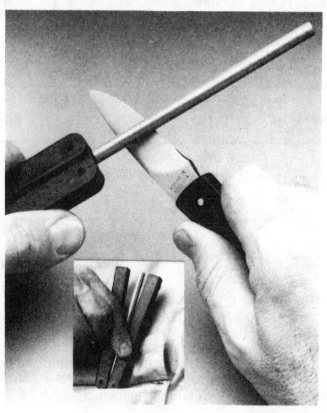

ELIMINATING THE WIRE

When you use a rough abrasive surface, you get an edge with rough segments sticking out on both sides of the edge. A medium surface removes most of those rough edges, leaving a few smaller ones to stick out on both sides. Finally, a fine stone brings your knife's edge into one continuous line. Result: the knife's edge line is continuous.

However, even though you may have a finely ground straight, razor-like edge, it may still have a wire, which is a liability for the cutting edge. Certainly, the wire fouls up a knife's edge retention. That's the reason for a slack belt fine sharpener. That's also the reason for stropping your knife's edge. Assuming, however, that you have neither of the above strops or slack belts, you have to remove the wire yourself.

First, understand what it is and how it develops on the edge of your knife. As you rub your knife's edge against the last (fine) abrasive surface, a tiny roll of steel forms on the opposite side of the edge.

Second, test for it. Drag your thumb nail backward along the opposite side of the edge you just ground on and feel your finger nail perhaps catch on the metal.

I was having lunch with Jerry Younkins, one of the knife writers in the U.S. He said, "Mike, (the owner of Blackjack Knives) is a genius." Blackjack knives come super-sharp out of the box. If you dull yours, they will sharpen it for free. Therefore:
NO WIRE!

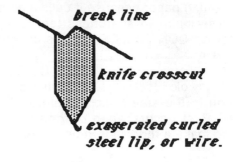

WIRE EDGE AFTER SHARPENING

break line

knife crosscut

exagerated curled steel lip, or wire.

Whether or not you know the wire is there, take it off. Change to a larger, bigger angle **on the fine stone** and go over the surface a few times on each side to make sure the edge is bare. Thus, if you put a 15 edge on your knife, switch to 20 degrees and finish with the fine rubbing surface at that angle. Use light pressure, and make sure to storke each side of the edge evenly along the complete cutting edge.

Another way to bring your blade's edge into perfection is by stropping it on your belt, or top of your boot. When stropping, draw your knife along the edge in the opposite direction. Move it with edge trailing, **not leading.** Don't slice into the leather by moving the blade along the surface with the edge in front. If you do, you'll cut into the leather. You are not trying to remove any more metal, just take away the rough edges the stone produced. A leather strop improves the edge on your blade because it takes off that fine wire. Incidentally, you can do the same thing better on the cardboard back of legal pads. Denim material also works.

I've never done this, but I plan to try. I am going to reload some abrasive powder into my twelve gauge shotgun and shoot my belt. I'll stand away—-ten, twenty and thirty yards—-and blast. When I can feel the abrasiveness on the surface of the belt, I'll know I have grit in my leather at the surface which means I've just barely penetrated. Then I'll oil my belt with Neatsfoot or Hubbards and wear the belt. From then on, I'll be able to pull my leather belt off my jeans in the woods, tie off the buckle on a tree and strop my knife as sharp as a commercial razor. I'll blast my big leather sheaths, too.

Test your knives for a sharp edge in several ways. I don't like cutting paper because it dulls a cutting edge. My favorite, always-employed sharpness test is to shave the top of my forearm. DON'T SLICE. That's cheating, and you could cut your arm.

RUSTY BLADES?

Many old blades are not stainless. They have a mixture of carbon in the steel, and therefore, the knives are prone to rust. Rust occurs when oxygen (in the air) combines with iron to make a reddish ferrous oxide.

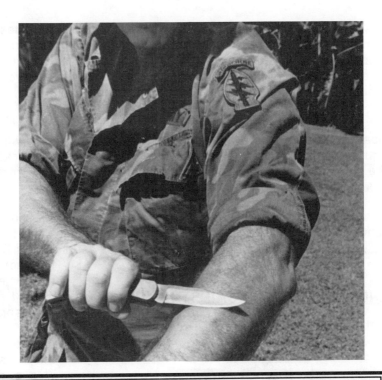

Shaving my arm. Create an edge without a wire, and run the blade straight down your arm without slicing. If your arm is bare after the blade passes, I guarantee, your knife will cut <u>something</u>.

Rust is blade enemy number one. It's the big enemy of most non-stainless blades and typically destroys the cheaper bolo knives and machetes, especially those made in Third World countries. Most of us look at the sides of our bolo knives and shrug at the rust we see. Perhaps we don't realize: just as the rust eats away at the side of the blade, it also penetrates and pits the cutting edge. That's why parkerized knives turn me off. You get a great looking knife out of the box that supposedly will never rust—-at least where you can see it. Then you rub off the parkerized finish at the edge—- the part of the knife you need to protect most from corrosion. You spend time to put a terrific edge on your blade and put it away. Then you go into the field and the edge is corroded and pitted so it won't cut beans.

Resharpen these by attacking the edge from both sides. Perhaps you'll need to use a file. Follow that with a coarse, medium and fine stone. For long term storage, heat up your blade over an open fire or perhaps in your home stove's oven, then sink the blade's edge into paraffin or candle wax.

Rusty knives often begin deteriorating under the handle. Heat the knife in your oven, and then apply some canning wax right at the junction of the handle/blade. The cooling off sucks the wax down into the cracks, and protects the tang from corroding and weakening.

When you sharpen big blades, you may find it more convenient to hold the blade steady and move the stone down the edge. To help hold the angle constant, mount the stone on a wood paddle with glue.

MAKE A PLYWOOD PADDLE
TO HOLD SHARPENING STONE
ANGLE CONSTANT AGAINST BLADE

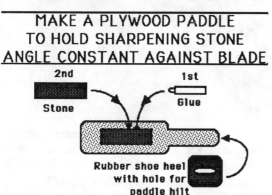

Folding knives require an extra bit of maintenance. You should keep the blade-pocket sanitary, especially if you use the knife to cut food. I use a toothpick with cloth or cotton wrapped around the end, and swab out that narrow area. Then I run fresh, hot water down into the slot. After that, I drip a very small amount of oil into the blade/handle junction, and the job is finished. With a clean blade and blade pocket, I know that my knife is All-American. On the other hand, use a blade dirty with petroleum base oil on your lunch meat and you will think you're Russian, 'cause you'll get the Trotski's.

Spend the time to keep your knives sharp, and use them only in that condition. Always leave them clean. That way, your knife work will be safer—- and surer.

Chapter 5

MAKING YOUR KNIFE
FEED YOU

The best use for your knives is food preparation. When you lack a knife, you'll have to use your teeth. With your knives, however, you can prepare a feast for "you, the king" of the woods. Your knife can make you happy, and you'll appreciate the tool most just about the time you burp.

Outdoor woods people eat better than city folks. That's one reason they stay healthy, live longer, and perhaps enjoy life more. Look at some of the food comparisons:

CITY PRESERVED	WOODS FRESH
Farm animals nourished on steroids and antibiotics.	Venison, rabbit, pheasant, fish, etc.
Sprayed fruit, waxed to look shiny.	Wild apples, coconut.
Frozen or canned vegetables.	Fresh tubers, salads.
Fast foods. * (greasy calories)	Fast. Don't eat. (no calories)

* Reason enough to live in the woods.

Bill Gothard reminds us in his *Basic Youth Conflicts* that God directed man to rest on the seventh day. "Perhaps," reasons Gothard, "we should do the same for our overworked digestive systems." I don't know about you, but I look into a mirror and see something resembling my government. On the front end, it has a voracious appetite and greedily consumes everything it can gobble up. On the other end, it creates pure waste.

> I don't want to admit I'm fat, though; I'm just a little short for my weight. I think 6'-11" would suit me better.

Think what good only a couple of days with a short food supply would do for our health! Unfortunately, if we don't have any food at home, we go out for some fried food——with a carbonated soft drink. Yuck! The cook probably thought we needed another oil change.

So look forward to dining out in the woods or jungle. It will be the best for you and the taste never misses, especially when you have the kind of hunger only outdoor life can provide. However, just as you can't eat out in the city without cash or a credit card, you can't dine out in the woods without at least one good knife. Think of the difference a knife will make in the two food columns below. With a knife, you dine on the foods in the left column. Without one, you encounter the foods on the right.

WITH KNIFE	WITHOUT A KNIFE
Meat	Hide, hair, guts.
Fish	Scales, head, fins, guts
Fowl	Feathers, beaks, claws
Vegetables	Peelings
Roots	Peelings

The kinds of meat you will encounter in the field will be vastly different from what you buy. As the world population grows and people become more affluent, they become picky eaters. Beef is the big deal. That's why the rain forests are disappearing——humans need space to grow beef so they can block their arteries faster. But just about any kind of meat you can bag in the field is edible. I've eaten a lot of the North American variety, including bear and rattlesnake. Still, there's more I haven't tried. I'm told that alligator tail is wonderful.

If you shoot one in Florida, however, it's a felony. Just as in Florida, crocodiles are protected in Australia, even though the salt water crocs take a few people a year (without a license, too). What is it about lawmakers who protect alligators and crocodiles? I think it's professional courtesy.

As you probably know by now, meat is prepared in two stages. The first occurs in the field, whether it's a farm animal or one which recently passed away from being overweight—due to an addition of lead to its carcass. We call that, "field dressing." It's an art form. Mess up in the field and you bring home something even a first-class chef will have trouble making tasty.

The second kind of knife work occurs in your kitchen. If you live in a shelter designed for the woods, jungle or farm, you ought to have a second kitchen for harvesting. For meat, it would be the place where your knives convert the field-dressed carcass to chops, steaks, roasts and ground meat. Also, take special note of jerky. In Oregon I raised about 500 rabbits and I carved and dried the back straps into some of the finest jerky anywhere.

To get the idea and practice a bit with your knives, buy whole chickens and cut them up before cooking. Turkeys will be a bit more difficult. Practice is a good idea, though, and you save money because whole birds are cheaper than those you buy cut up and pre-packaged.

FIELD DRESSING

Even if you don't hunt, you can save money if you buy a whole animal from a farmer. With your knives, you literally cut out the slaughterhouse, wholesaler and butcher mark-up on meat. If you go to an animal auction (just about every week in any rural community) and bid against farmers who know value, you'll be buying whole animals at the very lowest price. Ask for advice. Rural people are a lot friendlier than most city folk, and if you tell a farmer you want to buy an animal for taste, he'll most likely steer you away from the bull.

I've done several goats and sheep just that way, and the results have been extraordinarily good. If you're short on cash or freezer space, split an animal with a friend. Stake your animal out in your backyard and fatten it up. About a week before slaughter, feed the animal lots of fruit, the riper the better. When the animal's stool indicates the intestines are clean, pop it just behind an ear with a .22, and bleed it immediately. Just under the Adam's apple are two arteries. Insert your blade, cut left, then right. Hang the animal from the rear hooves and drain. That should remove all the blood from the meat.

Now comes the critical time in the life of any knife. You will use this thing to convert a bagged animal into a super meal. But there's a problem. It exists with big game and most fish. The first thing you have to cut with your knife is the toughest part of the game—either skin or hide. That dulls the blade for you, so you either have to resharpen or suffer because the rest of the cutting is slow and difficult, and somewhat dangerous.

You can fix this problem for a couple dollars. Buy a plastic box knife (metal is okay, but plastic is lighter and won't destroy your hand in temperature extremes). These knives come with a tough razor blade. Dull one end, flip them and use the new, sharp, other end. Each time you have to cut through hide, use the box razor. You can adjust how much of the blade is exposed so that you cut no deeper than you need to. When you get through the hide to the inside of the animal, you can switch to your regular still sharp knife.

Hang your animal from the **rear** legs. Spread the legs with a piece of wood and tie them off. Adjust your plastic box knife so that the blade will ONLY cut hide. Then cut around each lower leg—a circle, and from that cut straight down each leg to the rump. The next cut is risky. You want to make sure not to slice through the animal's belly hide into the intestine, because the leakage from the intestine will taint the meat with *E.coli* intestinal bacteria. Minimize the risk by adjusting the blade to the animal's belly skin thickness. Cut straight down the belly, starting from the poop-chute to the breast bone. If you don't cut all the way through the hide, that's okay. Change to a drop-point blade if you have one, and cut the same line again, from the inside out. You will rerun this cut as if it weren't there immediately.

Now slice from the inside out and cut only the hide, (very carefully) down the belly. If you made a box-knife cut, follow the same line. Don't get hair or wool on the meat. Use the two-knuckle blade hold to get in behind and cut outwards as you slide the blade down.

Skin back the belly a little. Wrist-flip the curved edge of your swept-up skinning blade knife into the crevice separating meat from hide and peel the hide away toward the sides. As soon as the hide is back—-out of your way and you have room to work, change blades to a smaller dropped point, and make a small incision through the transparent

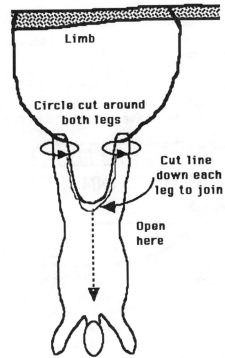

membrane (peritoneum) enclosing the entrails. Now, turn your knife so the blade faces you, protect the entrails with your fingers, and open up the abdominal cavity. Switch to a clip-blade pocket knife for penetration, and saw cut around the anus. Then tug on the lower intestine so to get it out whole. Tie off the end of that poop-chute to prevent tainting the rest of the meat.

Cut through the diaphragm, then reach through, down toward the head with a small blade and sever connecting arteries and wind pipe. Pull out the heart and lungs. That completes field dressing.

SKINNING THE CARCASS
Warm animals are easier to skin than cold ones. Warm rabbit fur will peel off easily, and a deer skin will do just about the same. Pulling hard on the deer skin with just about all my weight, I needed a skinning blade in only a few tough spots. If you have a long haul through areas where the meat could pick up dirt or flies, wait 'til you get home and count on skinning a cold carcass with a rounded skinning blade.

I left the hide on an animal I shot in Oregon once because I had to pull it up hill backward about a thousand feet. I sawed off a short viny maple limb, opened the mouth, inserted the limb, played dentist for a moment and had him bite down hard on it, then tied the snout tightly together. That way, I had a handle attached to the animal's strongest teeth. That was a long, difficult drag. Without hide on the carcass, I would've messed up a lot of hindquarter meat.

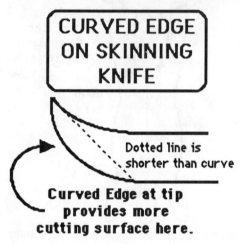

CURVED EDGE ON SKINNING KNIFE

Dotted line is shorter than curve

Curved Edge at tip provides more cutting surface here.

Make a circular cut around both legs, and then slice down each leg to make the cuts join at the rear. Use a round-edge skinning blade because of the long slices it takes. Tug hard on the hide to speed up the process. On a warm animal, you should finish in under ten minutes.

Cut the head. Leave a lot of neck meat on the body to grind up into meat patties later. Generally, the toughest meat on any animal is the tastiest. Take the four quarters off whole. Allow your knife to find the proper route to a ball-joint on each side. Saw the hooves if you are carrying up-hill for a long way and you want a little less weight.

With a big knife, cut around the back and through the flank meat. Catch the breast section in one hand as you cut through the last of the backbone meat that holds it. Later, you will slice through the ribs for a babecue.

Use a heavy blade to cut through the aitch bone or chop through it with a small camp axe. The aitch bone is the soft cartilage on the front side of the poop chute cavity. On an old animal, you'll have to smack it. Then spread the hind legs, and cut into the meat again toward the ball joints. When you cut the two hind quarters, the backbone section will drop into your hands.

ALL COOKING UTENSILS FURNISHED COURTESY OF PERSONAL KNIFE AND GOD

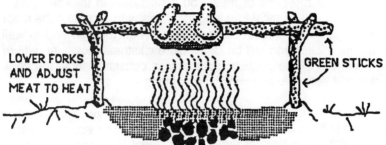

LOWER FORKS AND ADJUST MEAT TO HEAT

GREEN STICKS

If you're tactical, make drywood fire during daylight, which burns dow to hidden (in pit) coals for nighttime cooking. Angle the green stick through meat to get rare and well done. Don't use Hemlock wood or any other poison stick to hold meat. Wear an eyepatch over your shooting eye to prevent night blindness in case of attack.

Will you eat some of this in the field? With a thin blade on your pocket folder or a fillet knife, cut out the backstrap and cook it over coals. Cut up some dry hardwood and burn it down. Make

Chop a wide angled point on a thick limb with a MachAx, then narrow the angle toward the tip to put a barb on a spear point. Harden the green limb over coals. Then, fish and turn hot meat over.

Enlarged View Tip

Barb

75

the meat carrier adjustable so you can raise and lower the meat to control the cook rate.

In the Crocodile Dundee movie, Mick asks the woman, "How do you like your go-round." The question was in reference to rare or well done. If the hunk of meat you cook varies in thickness, as it does on the legs of most four legged critters, you can roast the meat over the coals on a level carrier stick. When the thin end is well done, the thicker part will be rare. On backstraps, however, where the thickness of the meat is more or less constant, angle the cook stick to get both rare and well done portions.

Even if your fire has burned down to a bed of hot coals, you can use your knife to cut small pieces of softer wood so you get a flame going. When the flame's upper end is meat-high, you contain the meat's juices.

Once you have four legs and a chest cavity, you're ready to go into the harvest part of the cutting. Generally, you'll do this at home in one of your kitchens, so your set of kitchen knives will be handier. A big (9 1/2") blade will provide straight cutting on the hindquarters to give you consistently thick meat for even cooking.

BIRDS

Meat eaters choose from a wide variety of four legged (two in Australia) animals, and dozens of birds. A knife doesn't help you much on a bird, but you **need** a big knife to make a device to field dress your birds as soon as they hit the ground. It's important, too. Though it isn't done much in this country, Germans usually apply this treatment because they know how fast bird meat taints. Besides, they just hit the bird with a load of shot, some of which perforated the intestines, so the bird is leaking you-know-what into the meat.

Cut and peel the bark off a green stick, and then insert it delicately into the bird's rear-most aperture. Once in, revolve the stick about half a dozen times. Upon extraction, you'll see the entrails from your feathered dinner wrapped around the stick.

If you're tactical, you may have to prepare your bird while on the move. Once you remove the entrails, work on the feathers.

76

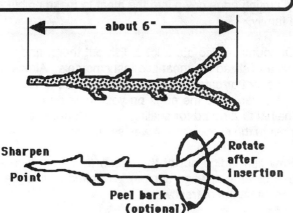

WOOD BRANCH TOOL FOR CLEANING GAME BIRD INNARDS

about 6"

Sharpen
Point

Peel bark
(optional)

Rotate
after
insertion

Note of course, if someone is chasing you, you'll leave a trail. (We show you how to double back and handle the people who are watching your feather trail in *Great Livin in Grubby Times*. The pin feathers burn off over an open fire. With head and claws chopped off, impale his plumpness on a green stick. No time to wait for coals? C&C it. (Cremate and chew) I recommend slower cooking, but as far as the gutting and de-feathering go, the same treatment will create great cuisine on just about any bird you bag.

OTHER FOODS

As you travel around, you'll encounter different foods to prepare with a knife. Are tubers safe? Can you eat Opossum? Basically, the best advice is to watch the natives, and eat what they eat. Make sure, however, to cook everything because your body won't adjust to their parasites and bacteria.

Recently, I moved to Fiji. I used one of my survival knives (6 1/2" blade) daily to feed my face with coconut. If you don't want to climb a tree, you can tie your knife to a long pole and reach enough food to feed your family for years.

Sharpen a green stick and bury its dull end in the ground. Then, jam the coconut slightly off center over the point and pry the husk off.

Use the back edge of the knife to crack open the hard shell. Since my clip curved upward on that knife, I merely pressed the curved cutting edge down into the meat to make edible slices for the whole family.

Of course, I also ate a lot of fish out there, and the same knife cleaned and sliced the meat into tasty morsels. Almost every kind of fish you shoot or catch will open up from front to rear on the bottom side. You can save the edge on your knife by using several bottle caps nailed to a board for scaling. After cleaning and scaling, wash off dinner in the same water it was swimming in.

Raw fish is fine out of the ocean (in most places—not Oahu because of large sewage dumps). Cooked well is the way to go if your fish came out of freshwater.

KEEP YOUR KNIVES SECURE
Try never to do anything which might put your knife in jeopardy. If you possibly can, don't use your knife directly on the food you prepare; use your knife to make another tool to do the work. If you break the tool, OK; make another. But if you break your blade, drop it into the water, or lose it, you have a problem. When tactical or in any hostile country, full of human or animal hazards, **never** lay your knife down or leave it unattended. Many people who broke this simple rule now reside in cemeteries. When you're working with a few knives and you lay them down on a tree stump, tie them together with a few feet of cord. Wherever you go, (overboard, under your canoe, into a foxhole, etc.) you want your knife with you. For security and your own safety, you need to learn to use your sheaths and holders as a matter of habit.

A sharp knife is the most important thing you can take with you in the woods. Without one, bagging any animal doesn't make much sense, unless you plan to chew on a lot of hide and hair.

Chapter 6

How to...
MAKE YOUR KNIFE MAKE

EVERYTHING YOU NEED OUTDOORS

Several branches of the military teach survival with nothing more than a knife. It may sound difficult when you think of parachuting into a jungle with only your knife (and perhaps a hidden spare) with you, but it can be done. Not only that, it can be done with style.

That's because your knife can be used to make the things that will keep you alive and living well, no matter where you go or what you do. Path Finder is considering a sequel to this book filled with the things you can make with your knives, such as:

Fire
Shelter
Traps
Outdoor tools
A solid bed and a stretcher
Clothing and footwear
Snoeshoes and packframes
Clothing
Packs and bags
Baskets, hats and snow goggles
Splints
Lots of weapons

Lose your knife, and you've lost a lot. That's why we teach you how to make one. We consider your knife to be **the critical item you must have** in order to be safe, secure and comfortable in the outdoor world.

Some Hollywood films narrow our thinking. We see the hero using his knife (drama, you know) **in** the trap rather than using it **to make** the trap. We see him **throw** his knife rather than use it to **make a weapon** and throw that. Don't believe Hollywood; keep your knife with you, always.

FOCUS ON THE CUTTING TOOL(S)

This thing called a knife is a very **precious outdoor tool**. Never risk losing it! Use it to make all kinds of implements, then go ahead and risk losing those. Why? With your knife, you can always make another implement, and the new replacement product will be better than the one you lost. Knives have uses as varied as your imagination will allow. Don't learn a trick way to use your knife; use your knife to make something that will do the trick you need. That's the best way to use this tool to its fullest.

You never look at a knife and think, "What a great stepping platform that would be to help me get up the face of a rock." What happens in real life, however, is this: You get into a tough spot and use your knife in the wierdest of ways to help you get it out. Sometimes, your blade suffers as a result. That's OK; with a good diamond sharpener, you can fix almost anything. Outdoorsmen wind up abusing their knives primarily because they come upon a situation where they need it **now** and have nothng else to work with. You can solve the potential misuse and abuse problems in a couple of ways:
1. Make a few utensils and short pieces of wire and wood you can use for a variety of common chores around camp.
2. Carry the right knife for the right job. You can use an abalone iron as a prybar, and an axe for heavy chopping. When you chose your knives, you probably acquired a variety of angles on various cutting edges. So you can chop or slice just by choosing the right tool. The multi-angled cutting edges on our PAKA are designed for those functions. Of course, the more you carry, the heavier you'll be weighted down.

Therefore, let's focus on method #1. First, we'll figure out how to cut some short pieces for making useful tools. To do that, you either have to saw or learn to cut things off evenly with your knife. In the chapter on choosing a knife, we told you to avoid a knife with saw teeth on the back of the blade. Without sawing ability, you'll still be able to cut through things evenly. Just roll the piece in front of you and tap on the back of the blade. To avoid having to go through that tedium and also to gain more versatility, add a wire saw to your inventory. They are light, don't take up a lot of space, and provide you with an extra increase in woods-ability.

Wire saws have been around for a long time now, and I recommend you carry one in your backpack. You can use these things to do some great tricks. In the simple catagory, saw off some branches. You can make handles for the wire saw itself, just for starters. If you're not tactical and you're cooking a lot, you can make pot hangers and long pot movers just to keep your hands free from burning. In super cold weather, you'll need to make a stone shovel or a handle to pick up the wire wrappings on hot stones. That way, you can build a helacious fire during the day and heat up some river rocks. At night, clear the ground, dig a trench under your tent, and shovel the hot river rocks into the trench to be covered with sand. Result: you sleep over radiant heat all night long. (See *Everybody's Outdoor Survival Guide*).

But suppose you need a clear path for a deadfall. You have all the ingredients of a great trap, tracks indicate your intended target passes over this piece of ground almost daily, and you have all the materials. Only one obstacle stands in your way—a branch from a large bent tree or bush is in the way of a clear falling log-bomb. That means the deadfall will be obstructed on the way down, and either deflected or slowed enough for your target to get out of the way. You can't get to the branch, however, unless you have a skyhook. Get a line up over the limb. Shoot it up there by tying it onto a slingshot projectile or an arrow, or— simply throw it. Once there, tie the saw onto it, tie another line on the trailing side of the saw, and use the lines to pull the saw back and forth until the limb drops and the bomb path for your deadfall is clear.

As long as we are teaching you some nifty things to do with your knife, we had better emphasize a few things **not to do.**

81

As we've said, throwing your knife is Hollywood junk. If your target is another human, and you either miss altogether or score with a poor hit, the knife may be returned to you, point first. Throwing it at an animal is even worse; 80% of the possible good hits will just cause the animal to run away and hide. Archers know what I mean. I personally have lost at least three dozen arrows this way.

For the same reason, don't use your knife in a trap. The animal will probably not be hit in a vital area and therefore break away— taking your knife along with it.

Unless you have a center point knife and a fair size spline, **Don't** use your knife for a prybar. I've seen too many broken blades. It most frequently happens when chopping a notch into a limb. You snap into the cut one way, then the other, but discover that the cuts don't meet each other, so the solution is to pry sideways with the blade. Uh-oh. You either took a visible chunk out of the cutting edge or bent it over in a way you could only see with a magnifying glass. Either way, the blade won't cut for you until you resharpen it.

For part of the research on this book, I spent an hour on the phone with Jerry Poletis, a custom knife maker. He explained that the harder the blade becomes, the longer it holds an edge, but—the harder it is to sharpen. Moreover, the metal becomes very brittle, or breakable. I interviewed metals expert A.B. Underwood of Carson City, and he told me this: If the Rockwell hardness of your knife's edge is so high that a file won't bite into it, there's a higher chance of the knife being brittle, and therefore snapping under severe stress.

Thus, if your knife has good edge retention, using it for a screwdriver makes no sense at all. When you try to turn the screw, you apply very sharp pressure at two extremely thin points on the edge of the blade. They snap off because the back up metal is on the top, not the sides. Then, with jagged holes in the blade's cutting edge, it just won't cut.

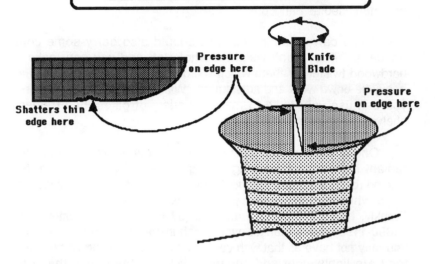

THE KNIFE AS A SCREW DRIVER MAXIMUM DAMAGE TO YOUR BLADES SENSITIVE EDGE

Pressure on edge here

Knife Blade

Pressure on edge here

Shatters thin edge here

Keep in mind that your knife is your most basic, most needed tool. That's why keeping it in perfect working shape and keeping it in your control are important. Do these two things, and you'll always be able to convert a wild animal into a wild meal. Moreover, you'll be able to make a wide variety of woods-tools and implements to make your outdoor wonderful.

Whole books have been written on the subject of shelter. We wrote on the subject, ourselves, in *Everybody's Outdoor Survival Guide*. (2nd edition) Of course, we went about it from a different viewpoint, and we explained the theory more than we explained the nuts and bolts of construction.

The old way of building outdoor shelters employed lashing, and in order to make anything substantial you had to carry a ton of rope with you, then cut it up into small pieces. Today, all you need to carry are some plastic ties; they're lightweight and tie things quickly.

The new-improved method employs plastic ties for a number of good reasons. The first has to do with our concept of weight-to-utility ratio. If an item is heavy and has little use, we give it a "one"

83

on a 1-10 scale. On the other hand, if an item can be well and widely used, but weighs almost nothing, it scores a nine or ten. Enough plastic ties to build a tree house won't weight down your pack. In addition, they are quick to use and strong. That's why they are often used as handcuffs.

If you carry plastic ties, you should also carry some coat hangers.   They don't weight a whole lot, and you can make a hardwood twister for them which will do quite a few tricks—both in heavy tie-down work and adjustment. With a bunch of coat hangers, you can use your knife to make a variety of gates, bed frames, shelves, and several other items.

One of the best uses for coat hangers is to provide you with radiant heat in your bedding during winter. If you sleep on the ground (bad idea; see *Hammock*) and you have to stay in the woods for a while during winter, you may want to sleep cozy warm. Frankly, I would rather use an MPI, (37 East St, Winchester, MA, 01890-1198) space blanket over a high insulation ground cover, but you may not have all that with you, even though you should because they are lightweight and cheap.   Without them, use the coat hangers.

Bed down high enough so rising waters won't bother you. Go down to the river and take out a bunch (dozen?) of flat, six inch river rocks. Wrap the rocks with coat hanger wire and leave a hook. Build a fire Satan would envy.   Place the rocks **in** the fire, hook up. Clear the area. (Sometimes steam pockets inside the rocks cause them to explode and make you holey.)   When you return, take the hot rocks out of the fire and lay them in a trench under your bed. Cover the rocks with three inches of soft sand. Lay down over the sand covered trench. If you use a sand pillow in a sturdy pillow case (like a sand bag) one of the hot rocks can rest inside. Will it be **real cold?** Make two trenches. Drink enough water to set your alarm clock (bladder) and take new stones out of the fire in the middle of the night for a second trench. Then move your corpus to the new location.

First, cut and package the coat hanger wire. Snap off the hanging loops and discard them.   A series of fair (not hard) taps on the back edge of your knife will knock it through and cut the wire cleanly.

Without a hardwood handle for twisting wire, you can use your knife handle. Make a twisting loop, sheath your knife, then insert the handle through the resulting hole, twist, and you can draw two objects together with amazing power. You can also adjust and take up the slack on any gate or door. Of course, hardwood will do this as well, and you won't have to worry about damaging your knife. If you have the time, you're always better off making a tool instead of using your knife recklessly.

While not the best for your knife, especially if the pommel or bolster is made of a soft metal, pounding nails improves your ability in the woods tremendously. Don't grab onto the blade. Sheath it first and hold onto the sheath.

Three feed sacks are better than two. With extra sacks, build a pillow.

With a heavy knife or a saw, you can sleep like a king in the woods. Teach yourself how to make a great, above-the-ground outdoor bed for less than a dollar. I doubt very much if any outdoor luxury beats a good night's sleep. In order to enjoy this, you need a knife that will cut and de-limb a couple of poles, along with spreaders that will push against feed sacks to make a firm, comfortable sleeping surface.

85

Next time you go into the woods, take three feed sacks with you at a cost of about a dime each. The key piece that makes this bed comfortable is the A-frame you make with your knife. When your body weight pushes down on the bed rails, the A-frame spreads them so they stretch the sacks out to the side and you sleep on a tight, supportive surface. It's as close as you can come in the woods to sleeping on a Sealy.

The sacks are not only cheap; they are lightweight and easy to pack. Once you make this bed, you won't have to sleep on the ground anymore. Therefore, you avoid many of the hazards found in jungles, and you need not worry about heat loss through conduction. No feed sacks? Use the large size hammock we featured in our hammock book. Hook the hammock rails to the wood rails and cut a larger A-Frame.

With weight clamped on to your knife and the thong attached through the new hole in your knife's pommel, (see Chapter 2 on modifying your knife), you can notch two logs quickly. When you chop with your knife or your machax, it's a good idea to drop down on one knee the same way Boy Scouts teach you to do when using a camp axe. That way, wild swings hit the dirt before they hit you. Also, remember to keep the knife blade plane aimed so it's not in line with your body. Cross the two pieces you cut at the notches, and simply yank them together with a plastic tie. Whether you're building a lean-to or a frame structure to hold thatching, you can lay out a whole wall on the ground, then notch and plastic-tie the pieces together in no time at all.

Some outdoor people like fine cuisine on the trail. They make macaroni and cheese for dinner, then cheese and macaroni for breakfast. If you live in the outdoors and use pots and pans, most of them will have wire suspension handles that flop down and heat up in the fire. Cut a long, green, tree limb and trim it to use as a pot holder. Trim the bark on the part of the limb under which the pot will hang. That will keep burnt bark from dropping into the stew.

The woods contain some of the finest cuisine in the world. You can make a great meal over open coals from just about anything that walks, flies, swims, or even crawls. The meat is pure; it contains no steroids and little animal fat. The taste is marvelous.

For fresh camp meat roasted over coals, make a good size fire out of dry wood about an hour or so before sunset. When the fire is down to coals, set a green pole across the pit, and roast dinner. You'll be starved. Use your largest blade to lop off the cooked portions on the outside layer.

Speaking of fire, a knife makes one a lot easier to start. Make a dry piece of solid wood into a flaky "fuzz stick." Result: you kick off a good blaze in a hurry. In *Everybody's Outdoor Survival Guide*, we tell you how heat leaves your body and how best to get it back in there. Without a good knife, though, the job will be a lot tougher.

To harden green wood, whittle it to a sharp edge and cook it over hot coals. Thus, you make durable tent stakes and a spear with a point that penetrates. Be careful; don't let your spear catch fire. Just heat it until it smolders. Also, if you can, quench it—stuff it into cold water to cool it off. That seems to help harden it better.

Reasonably decent arrows will also harden over the same fire. Make a dozen. Keep the best for shooting, and cut the others off short to use in traps. When you need a certain size piece of wood in a certain shape, use your knife as a draw knife. Turn the blade at approximately a 45° angle and pull on the handle as well as the tip of the blade. With your one hand on the handle, regulate the angle of the blade so you don't bite too deeply into the wood. That's one reason we choose the Ghurka Kukri as the big blade to carry. On soft wood, such as cedar, you can turn that blade upwards and scrape a nice round surface on your arrows.

Softwood arrows can be trued gradually by turning them in forked sticks and peeling them. Cedar trues easily and flies fast because it's light. Because it is so soft, however, you need to think about attaching a harder point. Hardwood points are OK, but obsidian rock, which comes out 300 times sharper than a razor, is best. Press down hard with all your weight on alternate sides to shape the two sharp edges; then set it in a notch and tie it off. If you have glue. . .

Almost everybody who traps uses snares. To make one yourself, you put the whole trap together with pieces you make with a knife. You can increase the efficiency of a flat ground snare if you add a net to the draw string. That's especially true when you are so hungry you wait around to spring the trap yourself. The added net decreases your chances of fasting.

With time and patience, you can make a good, straight bow. Carve the bow and reverse-stress it over heat. After it sets up, bend it backwards and string it.

In Book II of *Everybody's Outdoor Survival Guide*, we devoted a whole chapter to handmade weapons. Almost all of those could be made with a good knife.   Just remember—-the ends of those weapons facing the customer get a pointed end; and the ends on your side stay blunt.

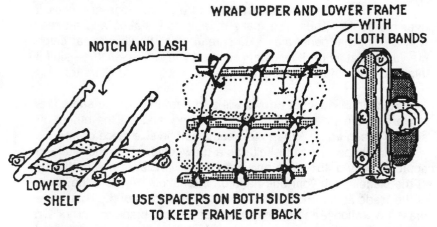

WRAP UPPER AND LOWER FRAME
WITH
CLOTH BANDS

NOTCH AND LASH

LOWER SHELF

USE SPACERS ON BOTH SIDES
TO KEEP FRAME OFF BACK

For carrying a heavy load, build a packboard. Cut all the cross members first, and then lash them together with small plastic ties. You can extend the bottom shelf out as much as 6 inches and support it from the top of the frame.

If you get caught in snow unexpectedly, protect your eyes with a knife-hewn pair of snow/sun goggles. Make the slits first to insure that your chosen piece of bark is workable. Dry bark will split. Green bark will make a good pair of eye savers. The trick is in keeping the sight-hole tiny, and rounding the edges to keep the bark from splitting when it dries.

Snowshoes are also a great idea if you get caught in a big storm. If you have a pot, steam the green wood members to bend the way you need them. You prop the curved portion out with green sticks, and cook (carefully) the whole snowshoe to harden it in place. After that, you can drill or notch the shoe frame to receive the support strings.

Rawhide will be abundantly available if you live in the woods. All the animals wear it, and it never goes out of fashion. So, while roasting dinner, save your hide by using theirs. Of course, make belts and straps and a tumpline. Use a straight edge to make sure you get a straight cut. A leather drilling blade, found notably on most Swiss Army Pocket Knives, will put the proper holes in the leather strapping.

Some girl told me when I was a teen that only two things kept me from dancing well—my feet. The same two things will keep you from operating in the woods—unless you take care of them.

Given a long-term outdoor survival situation, the shoes on your feet may not last. In another book, we teach you to go into the field with three pair of *Hi-Tech* boots. One of those pair must be able to operate in water without deterioration. Footgear is frequently ruined around water, so you should think about using your knife to make a pair of moccasins. Jeremiah Johnson, the famous 6' 4" mountain-man who lived and survived in the late 1800's, described how he made his moccasins. He used his knives to make two for each foot. The inside was soft and pliable; the outside was made from the thick rump hide of a large animal. History records that his powerful legs could deliver a respectable kick, and that his hard-shelled moccasins were the leading edge of that weapon. He made his point several times.

You can do the same. Tan the hide of a young animal with the hair on. Make patterns out of trash material, (newspaper, rags) to fold around your foot and the top of your ankle comfortably. Then use those fitted patterns to outline the cut on the animal hide. The resulting forms fold around your foot. Don't lap the edges—butt them to one another. Use both leather glue and good nylon thread for stitching.

Once this inside glove for your foot is complete, prepare another for the outside. First, though, think about insulation. The best today is Thinsulate, but you may not be able to locate any.

Probably what you will have available, however, is pre-formed solid packing and little peanuts made of Styrofoam used for all kinds of shipping. Slice these and glue together a mosaic pattern all around the mossasins you just form fitted to your foot.

It's best to use a different pattern for the outside moccasin layer. When the stitched and glued joints aren't superimposed, you build in more water resistence. Use the rump hide from a large animal, again with the hair on the outside.

TOOLS MADE WITH YOUR KNIFE

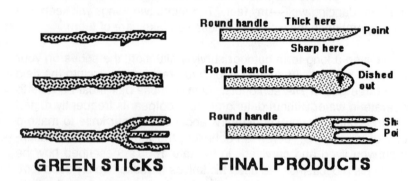

GREEN STICKS   FINAL PRODUCTS

Use your knife to carve eating utensils, preferably out of hardwood. Even if you peel the bark off a sharpened green twig and use it only as a fork, you won't have to eat hot food with dirty hands which can spread bacteria all over your dinner. Whittle a whole set of utensils from hardwood. Be careful not to use a poison wood. Throw some sandpaper in your rucksack to keep splinters from coming off and winding up in your dinner.

The primary utensil you need to make comes from green hardwoord. It's a straight branch about four feet long and one to two inches in diameter. The end of the branch closest to the trunk is the working end. Leave one or two side limbs attached to the main stick. You can slip these over a pot handle and lift anything attached to a coat hanger. You can also use this piece as a fishing spear. Jam it through a fish and the barb holds it on the end for you.

Cut a 2" limb off a tree. Chop a wide angled point on a thick limb with a MachAx, then narrow the angle toward the tip to put a barb on the spear point. Harden the green limb over coals. You can use this as a cooking tool or a fishing spear.

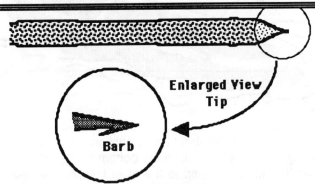

Enlarged View
Tip

Barb

Sharpen the end to a fine (20° or less), point. **Barb the point,** preferably on two sides. Harden that point over coals. In addition to being a useful weapon, you can spear meat on a grill with it and turn it over, or haul it out of the fire to a wooden plank plate.

Likewise, you can rig a turning spindle, and use the curved edge of your knife inside a block of wood to make a bowl or two. Then, with a carved spoon, you're in stew heaven. Likewise, carve a second knife out of hardwood, and it will be useful for cutting softer items, such as bread.

For a great fish trap, you need your knife and a hammock. Use your knife or axe to trim the branches off the tree you choose to spring load. Climb the sapling tree (should be about 6-15 feet high, and tie off the top. Pull the tree down and tie it off to an anchor. Lay your weighted hammock flat on the bottom of a water pool with a loose line attached through the loop on both ends. Wait until dinner swims over the net; then cut the tie-down. To feed more than yourself, double the recipe.

Sooner or later, a pack with shoulder straps will come in handy. I like mine with an extra carrying strap so that I can move it easily. I prefer two of them. The large backpack moves your complete outdoor household goods. Inside that pack is a smaller daypack, which you use for field trips and hunts lasting less than a day long.

Around water, think about transportation. You can dig a log out to make a decent canoe. Since the bottom of any log is round, you will need an outrigger—tied to the main hull with two wood poles, like the ones on the Hawaii 5-0 TV series.

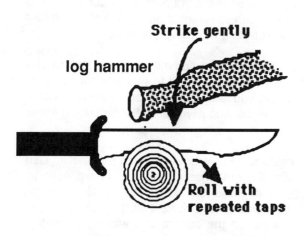

Strike gently

log hammer

Roll with repeated taps

If you don't have a saw and you need to cut brances of wood, use the Jerry Younkins chisel technique. Roll the limb you need to cut and tap on the back of your blade to sink it ever deeper into the wood. Then snap it apart.

Kept clean and sharp, you and your knife can make an abundance of outdoor goodies, and you can not only survive, but live in relative comfort—anywhere.

Chapter 7

DESIGN FACTORS IN BLADES

Since we first published this book, knives have grown to be regarded as subjects of high concern for outdoorsmen. Also, more knives are now on the market. To learn how to choose the best, it's a good idea to learn about:

Size, Shape, Material, Grind, Edge Angle, Tang, Finish, Heat treatment, and finally, cross sectional geometry.

Size is obvious. If you become a 4-blade owner, then you will choose a variety of knives so that the range runs from nine inches or over, down to two.

Shape of the blade has a lot to do with point location, as far as knife utility is concerned. Center point, or, spear point knives have strong spines. Given old materials, lots of steel in the middle of the blade gave it strength to stand against side flex. With the new steels out today, however, you can get a clip blade which will hold up as well as an old carbon steel center spine blade.

Material. Recently, 440-C stainless was the hot material, and most savvy knife buyers asked for it. The latest and greatest now, however, is ATS-34. In over a dozen knives recently tested under the toughest of use and abuse circumstances, it closed the gap between carbon and stainless in cutting proficiency."

93

Grind. Blade grinds come in one of four flavors: Flat, saber, hollow and semi-hollow. It goes like this: On a cheap knife, your grind will eventually become flat because most sharpeners are flat stones or straight rods. Expensive, specialty knives feature a slack-belt ground edge which provides the cutting surface with lots of back-up metal. Hollow ground knives come off a grinding wheel. To maintain that hollow grind, you may be tempted to use a grinding wheel. **Don't.** Too much heat could ruin your knife, and modern grinders turn so fast that heat control is a problem. Blackjack (and some other manufacturers) will sharpen their customers' knives <u>for free for life,</u> and their knives hold an edge like you wouldn't believe anyway.

Edge Angle. The gamut runs from 10 degrees to 40 degrees. In the last chapter of this book, we allow you the right to use our copyrighted plan for the PAKA, the Pivot Action Knife Ax. That knife incorporates three different angles in the blade because the blade is designed to do a lot of different chores.

Ten degrees allows you to hone a finer cutting edge on your blade, but it won't hold up under pressure. Conversely, a forty degree angle has a lot of metal meat behind the cutting edge, so the back-up keeps an edge together, even while chopping. But then, the fat forty degree guy **cannot** be honed to the fine edge a narrow angle can.

Go for a wide angle if you will use the knife to chop. Go for a more narrow angle if you want the knife to cut. Could somebody please build a blade with a narrow angle that would hold when you tapped the back of the blade through the wood? Somebody did. Blackjack's finish angle is only thirteen degrees, so the thing slices like a razor. It also chops and holds up under the chopping because of the slack-belt grind and heat treatment.

Tang. This is the part of the knife which extends back, through the handle material. A few years back, I would have told you to buy a knife with a full tang. But, today, new steels can make smaller tangs just as strong. Therefore, you can save some weight with a smaller tang and also buy a knife with a handle which will insulate your hand from electric current.

Finish. I never voted for plating until I talked with Mike Stewart at Blackjack. Some of his knives are plated so well that only the micro-edge protrudes. Since they resharpen knives for free anyway (they even pay for return freight), that a plated knife might be a great idea. Then, all you have to worry about is a thin coat of oil (Pro-Tech) on the cutting edge. Don't apply the oil with your finger. Drop some on a rag or cleaning patch and gently push the cutting edge into it.

Heat treatment. It's difficult for the consumer to find out how the knife was heat treated. You just have to go pretty much by the way your knife retains its edge. The latest and greatest way to go is to reduce the blade's temperature down to freezing levels. Blackjack knives does this with a special freezing process, and therefore the molecules of metal are more free to reallign in their strongest configuration.

Cross sectional geometry. If you cut your blade in half, you'll see the true shape of the blade. Mike Stewart from Blackjack told me he learned that a knife's cutting capacity, edge retention and overall performance is determined by this one factor. He said, "Mess up either way by only 4%, and you lose 20% or more of the knife's ability." Since, you can't cut a knife in half, you have to judge by performance. My personal Mamba is unbelievable. Jerry Younkins literally tortures his knives and has made his Mamba successfully do things which make me shudder.

Knife manufacturers have done all the experimenting and testing. By now they know what works and what doesn't. Some of them have spent thousands of dollars trying out one new idea. One knifemaker (Buck) has simply turned to prayer and been rewarded, so well in fact, that his business is reportedly worth 30 million dollars.

Even though Buck made some business moves that should have hurt him financially, somehow, his company is highly successful. Over a million Buck knives are sold annually. Some say Buck's secret is in annealing treatment. (Buck says it's in a kneeling treatment; he prays, God blesses.) There was a time when Al Buck's knives were constantly featured in an ad showing a Buck being driven through a bolt.

95

Buck recently joined forces with Wenger to make the SwissBuck. Some of the tools on that knife are more useful than those you would find on a Swiss Army knife. For example, the SwissBuck has a pair of pliers.

Two other highly successful pioneers in knifemaking are Lynn Thompson of Cold Steel and Mike Stewart of Blackjack Knives. Both make more expensive, specialty knives instead of the less expensive, high production, factory products. In Juneau, Alaska, I interviewed the owner of the Bullet and Blade Shop. He told me, "Alaska's climate and rugged terrain put a knife to ultimate use, so you absolutely need blade excellence." Cold Steel, (Ventura Calif) is famous up there where the last barrier of defense between man and mother nature is a good knife that won't fail you. Blackjack's knives are guaranteed unconditionally.

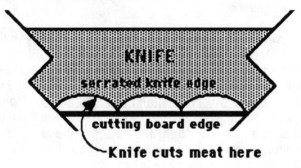

Finally, consider a knife with a serrated edge. Even in theory, it was a great idea. Thanks to SpyderCo, dreams have become a reality, and the serrated edge has earned its very own place on earthly hunting grounds. Since the cutting edges are round, you get more edge cutting per linear inch of blade than you would on a straight edge. Also, the points between the edges keep them from touching anything other than what you are cutting.

Granted, you don't have a wide choice in many of the above knife features because the manufacturers don't print all the relative information on their blades or in their packaging. You get what you pay for in this trade, however. American knife manufacturers are making the best in the world, in my opinion, and the specialty knife makers are on top of their craft.

Chapter 8

THE DOMINATORS:
SIZE AND SHAPE IN BLADES

You can live with the wrong grind, high carbon steel (it will rust), a softer metal, (you will have to sharpen it often) and a grind that's not the best. But the correct blade size and shape have to match the type of work you intend the knife to do.

Prove it to yourself by visiting a slaughterhouse, where the quickest butchers in the world use between 6 and 9 different blades within minutes. Don't we all wish we had a rack of sharp knives next to us every time we shot dinner? Instead, many us tough it out with just one blade. How well we tough it out is pretty much determined by blade size and shape. You don't need to do this; you can own several knives so that the variety covers you in every situation.

THE SIGNIFICANCE OF BLADE SIZE

"The bigger the better." That's the general rule. Blades generally run from three to eight inches. Some are even bigger, of course, but then you are talking more about a bolo knife or a machete.

Although big blades will slice and cut through cartilage with ease, they just can't get into little spaces and make fine cuts. So, carry both a smaller blade and a larger one. If you will go to the trouble of carrying four knives, you can have all the big-blade benefits plus the added utility you get from several smaller blades. Match up your hunting knife with either a pocket knife or a folding belt knife and you'll have the utility of a crafty meat cutter.

97

BIG BLADE BENEFITS

Small blades for combat are like BB guns in war. They're OK—as long as you can run like a deer. But a knife war is a life war and you had better increase your life insurance. You do that with a bigger blade. Why? The critical element in all combat is range. That's why swords were invented. The modern answer to range improvement for combat is handgun.

Anyway, the bigger the better. For those of us who only hunt to eat, a big blade quickly converts wild game to great eating food. At this writing, new steels for big blades give then super edge retention. One big blade, sharpened and properly and cared for, will last a long time in the field and perform a lot of work for you.

Of course, shape is also important. This is where it's at—the heart of the subject. If you have the best material, a fine grind, the perfect edge angle, and a big knife, but your blade shape is wrong for you and what you do, you'll struggle in the field.

Different blade shapes give a knife different utility. From time forward, just about all the changes in knife design have wrapped around blade shape. (That's primarily why we wrote this book: We saw other changes that could advance the knife into the 21st century.)

As any knife-maker will tell you, whatever you gain by changing the blade to perform in one way will decrease its ability to perform in another. Point location is a key factor, because it determines function. But it's a give-and-take proposition. Your blade loses one function-ability when you gain another by choosing a different point location. You can own a knife with the knife's point:

√ Dropped down, in line with the cutting edge
√ In the center of the blade for strength and penetration
√ On top in line with the blade's back edge
√ Above the blade's back edge so you achieve a curved underside for skinning

A drop-point blade is great for field dressing big game. However, drop point blades don't provide a sweeping, curved edge, so the blade won't skin very well. That's OK though, the hide is

God's way of keeping the meat clean 'til you get it home unless you live and hunt in warm country. In warmer temperatures, get the skin off right away and let the carcass cool out to help preserve the meat longer.

A center point knife most often has a stronger rib down the center so it can be used successfully as a pry bar. Center point knives are also good for combat, because they often come with both sides of the blade edged. Most daggers are center point knives.

A raised point knife employs that sweeping curved edge that skinners love. The higher the point, the more room you have to upsweep a generous curve at the tip of your knife. But gutting a deer without piercing the intestine is difficult with a raised-point knife. Use our two-finger hold if a raised-point is your only hunting companion. Otherwise, when you open the animal, you stand a good chance of piercing intestines and making a mess of the meat.

Until we discovered the new uses for a knife in the field, we were pretty much in favor of the dropped point. That's all changed now. Any knife will cut—somehow, but only a raised point does all the navigation and clinometer tricks we have come to love so dearly. Point location for our woods tricks is best when you can drill the quillion and use the tip of the knife like a rifle peep sight.

Of all the big blades to carry, consider the Gurkha Kukri. The shape of the blade provides excellent field utility, and you can use that knife to clear dense brush as well as for defense. It's also good for chopping wood and branches, which means it can help you fabricate shelter in a hurry. The main advantage to this knife is its dropped, curved skinning edge on the front. Of course, it skins well because of that curve at the point, but the dropped curve continues upward to the plain cutting edge. Therefore, it makes an excellent chopper because you strike the target with an angled blade. Recent tests in the *American Survival Guide Magazine* report that the Kukri will perform better than a hatchet for chopping. Not bad.

With that knowledge in mind, I toured the SHOT (Shooters, Hunters and Outdoor Trades) SHOW, where over 5,000 exhibitors of every kind were on hand to show their products and explain how they work. Enter Ethan Becker, knife designer for some of Blackjack's knives. He designed their Machax, which to me is an improvement over the original Kukri because of the blade's curvature. I asked him how he arrived at the curve, and I thought he would give me some great calculus formula. Instead, he told me, "I merely went out and tried blades I built with lots of different curves until I found one that would out cut all the others."

So often, what works in theory won't do diddly in the field. Becker must know this. What I find with his cure, however, is that his blade is shaped so that almost all strikes land on the target with the blade at a slicing attack angle rather than a straight-on collision. The result: his knife slices into the target.

NOTE THIS! If you decide to carry a Machax, be careful. Since the blade centerline curves up, then down around the handle, it could conceivably come back around on you. Also, if you swing this blade sideways and use a lanyard from the pommel hole looped around your wrist and the heavy weight makes you lose your grip, the blade could get out of control.

You can solve much of the danger problem by chopping with it so that the blade is never in line with your body. Most people hold an axe or the Kukri so that the handle is in line with the arm, which means the blade is in line with the body. **No-no.** Hold the handle firmly with thumb under, four fingers over, so that all your knuckles are directly over the tang. Thus, the handle extends across the body out front at a 45 degree angle. When you chop that way, you can rotate your wrist with a much better range of motion, and you can whip with your arm for much improved striking power. Also, with your knuckles directly over the tang, your grip improves so you stay in control. Finally, if disaster occurs and the thing slips out of your hand, the blade will fly off to your side, rather than swing down and make you holier than you were created.

The Becker Machax makes more sense to me than a camp axe because it performs better as a chopping tool. Without excessive head weight, it's lighter than a camp axe, and balanced better. Excess head weight always creates control problems.

This blade chops well because of the blade's curvature. It skins well, too. You merely hold the back of the blade and flick your wrist so the blade slices the hide away from your animal. You can throw (we don't recommend throwing) this effectively; the head weight will provide more time with blade forward as it rotates forward, and my model has both sides of the point sharpened. The blade stabs (which is great if attached to a pole). Finally, you can use your Machax as a draw knife because of its inside curve.

Given a choice between a great bowie or a large blade, I like the Machax because of its utility. Taking one into the field means you don't have to have such a large blade on your second sheath knife, and you could sharpen your second with a narrower (say, 15° edge for super sharp and fine cutting applications).

Probably the Machax would be the best blade you could own for hasty shelter or trap construction. Because of it's shape and balance, I think it will out-perform any machete. Incidentally, mine, out of the box, shaved my arm with ease, which tells me they took the time to fine grit grind the edge with a slack belt to bring it up like a razor.

If you decide to go into the field with this, as I have, do slide a section of bicycle inner tube over the handle. It's a full tang knife, and the inner tube will protect your hand from temperature extremes. Also, in the event you will be working around electricity for any reason, cover the tang both top and bottom with double layers of electrical tape before you slide the inner tube in place. If your hand can work over a bigger grip, wrap parachute cord between the handle and the inner tube.

With smaller knives, one small thing to add: Look for a good choil. It will help you to change grip enough to do some fine cutting, especially upside down.

YOUR BLADE'S EDGE
More and more, you see serrated edges appearing on knife blades. SPYDERCO produces the clipit, and they make a superb knife. Cold Steel also produces a small, kraton-handled serrated edge. Remember how cutting cardboard dulls your knife? Thompson put one out at the show and let people cut cardboard with it all day long. At the end of the day, the edge still held its own.

Buck now offers a knife with a whole series of blades which attach to the handle. Some of those are also serrated. Tests prove that serrated blades hold an edge three to seven times longer than ordinary edges. A few knife testers tell me that some of the serrated edges have done even better than that. Even if you have a kit, however, sharpening one of these blades in the field could take some time and expertise.

Once you have chosen the blade shape that will perform for you best, think about edge retention. You want your knife to stay sharp. Even if you accidentally dull your blade, however, a diamond impregnated rod and perhaps a leather belt impregnated with lapping compound could keep you sharp in the field for months.

As we discussed, the smaller the angle used in sharpening, the less metal you have backing up the cutting edge. If you shape your edge with a fat angle, such as 30° or more, the edge will hold better. Of course, a fat-angle edge like that won't cut as well as a fine 10° edge.

A high quality, (440-C) stainless will hold an edge better than a soft steel with a low carbon content. Hardness of the blade is most important when you think of edge retention. If your blade's edge is hard, though, it's much more difficult to put an edge on it. That's one big reason why we recommend diamond sharpeners. With the new steels, you just about have to go that way if you don't want to grow old while putting an edge on your knife.

If you want to find out how hard your knife edge is, run a file over the metal. Soft steels, such as those found on most machetes and axes, will allow the teeth of the file to bite in and take off metal. On the contrary, a file slides over hard steels without biting in.

After the blade is chosen, pay attention to the handle, including the pommel and quillion. We show you how in the next chapter. With a perfect (for you) handle on the ideal blade, you and your knife will be hard to beat, and the two of you should enjoy a long and useful life together.

102

To be able to use a knife well, the handle has to be correct. Sorry, very few knives are made today on which the handles can cut the mustard. Knife makers produce their products with handles too small, too short, a pain-inducing quillion, and no thumb rest to press for leverage. Worse, they produce metal handles or leave metal hardware and the tang exposed through wood or plastic to come in contact with your skin. Result, you burn your hand in the summer desert, or leave part of your hide in Alaska during January. To get handles to work best for you, fix them yourself.

Chapter 9

GETTING A HANDLE ON HANDLES

Your knife handle has to perform for you in certain ways that manufacturers often overlook. I blame the Europeans. Not those living today, but the ancestors of many Americans. Those Europeans were just as proud back then as we are today. But, they didn't drive fancy cars, they carried flashy knives around. Since the handle was always visible, they adorned it and showed it off to impress people.

To carry on in the great tradition, maybe we ought to produce a knife handle with a great looking hood ornament.

We're still plagued with the show-off syndrome today. Handles are made for looks, not function. Even when a hunting knife is carried in a full sheath, knife makers focus on how the handle looks, rather than how it performs.

Maybe this is the problem with knifemakers: when they deal with a knife, it has a freshly sharpened edge in a heated or air conditioned factory office. They just slept all night. They sit in a comfortable chair with enough light so some OSHA bureaucrat doesn't give them a citation. Their hands are warm and dry.

Not you, cowboy. You get cheap seats, terrible working conditions, and few government workers go where you just arrived because they're too fat. When you grip the knife handle, your blade is dull so you have to push it. Your hands are so cold you stick them into the warm animal you're working on to un-stiffen your fingers. You're sled-dog tired; you're working in the dark, and you've got slippery stuff all over the handle, which you <u>hope</u> is the animal's blood.

Yes, designers of handles and we, the users, face a different set of circumstances. The manufacturers ought to learn that, and make some practical improvements. Just ask yourself, what is this end of the knife supposed to do?

<u>How about . . .</u>
Fit your hand? (**At least!**)
Refrain from burning your hand in Arizona's August or freeze-drying your hand on contact in Delaware's December.
Keep your hand from sliding around, especially forward onto the blade?
Attach to a pole and become a spear?
Contain useful survival goodies?
Contain a cannister of mace for long distance perpetrator persuasion?
Perform like a hammer or chipper?
Attach to a thong?
Contain a pen light with a small light rod so you have a beam at the end of the knife's tip when you squeeze?
Insulate you from electrical shock?
Float if the knife will be used over water?
Contain pre-drilled holes at the back end to attach to extensions, so you could use it over fire?

This isn't an all inclusive list, either, but most knives today don't do any of the above. Only recently, since Rambo made us believe

Special Forces could walk on water, have we seen the arrival of "survival knives." Some of the handles on those knives will serve a portion of the above purposes.

But how about a knife you can hold on to? Of all the shortcoming of today's knives, none is worse than the failure of the manufacturers to make a handle to properly **fit your hand.**

If you play tennis, you know that racquet-makers produce different sizes to fit different player's hands. However, most knife handles are apparently made for Pygmies. The result: you get more control when playing tennis than you do in a struggle for life.

HOW TO DETERMINE HANDLE'S CORRECT SIZE FOR YOUR HAND

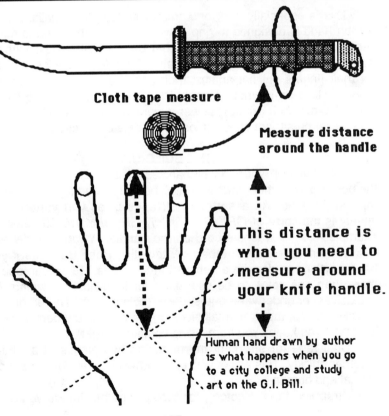

Cloth tape measure

Measure distance around the handle

This distance is what you need to measure around your knife handle.

Human hand drawn by author is what happens when you go to a city college and study art on the G.I. Bill.

What's absolutely critical is this: You have to be able to grab your knife and squeeze the handle hard. How can you do that when you wrap your hand around the handle and your fingers jam into your palm?

Generally, knife handles need to be built up. Before deciding what to use for the build up, figure out how fat your handle should be. Here's how. Use a ball point pen against a straight edge across the palm of your hand. Draw two lines criss-cross to make an "X" near the center of your palm. Measure the *distance* from the X out to the end of your extended middle finger. (Note for women: Measure to the end of your middle fingernail.) That *distance* should be slightly more than, or equal to the measurement around the handle of your knife. Any measurement less than that *distance* will lessen your gripping ability.

This is especially true for women with long fingernails. The human hand is designed to grip down best when the hand is made into a fist. But women can't do that on a small handle without jamming their fingernails into their palm. Therefore, they instinctively lay their fingers out flat against their palm so that their fingernails point back at their wrist. Result: they lose 60% of their gripping power. Since their gripping power is generally weaker, 40% of their own power puts them at risk of losing their knife in a struggle.

THE BUILD-UP

Let's build up your knives' handles. If tape is your choice for the build-up, use more than one kind, because you may need to use tape in the field. An assortment of tapes gives you variety, and variety is the spice of *GREAT LIVIN' IN GRUBBY TIMES.* Just for example, use: Parachute cord on the handle. Wrap it tightly and neatly, then cover it with tape. Automotive Hose Bandage if you have anything to do with a vehicle in the woods. Electrical tape in more than one color, to be used later for identification, wiring (for explosives) or underwater grip surface, (pole spear). Try red or pink bicycle reflector tape. A small piece on the back of the person's cap in front of you keeps you from losing contact at night.

Duct tape for strength and attaching two pieces of anything together quickly. This works well on dried wood used for traps, both animal and human.

Strapping tape (Scotch), for taping together things you don't want to tear apart under stress, such as your knife handle to a long pole.

Gripsy (available in any tennis shop) for the last, outside layer, to provide a sure, positive, comfortable hand-hold.

Consider using parachute cord for part of the build-up. In Hawaii, I've shot fish for years using tape over parachute cord on my pole spear to help prevent my hand from slipping. With tape on your knife handle, you can always remove it and use the cord if the need arises.

If you want to form fit the handle to your hand, another good way to go is with plastic wood.   Some manufacturer should experiment with an inflatable handle. A can of foam similar to insulation foam could blow the handle up—-into the customer's grip perfectly. The foam would then set up to become rigid. Result: light weight and custom fit.

You need sticky rubber on the handle. The commercial name for the stuff is Kraton, and Cold Steel features it on many of their knives now. The friction between the rubber and your hand insures that you'll keep positive control and that you won't drop it.

IMPROVING YOUR HANDLE WITH A SUPER GRIP SURFACE

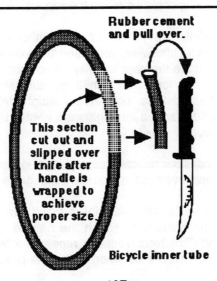

Rubber cement and pull over.

This section cut out and slipped over knife after handle is wrapped to achieve proper size.

Bicycle inner tube

A cheap way to cover the whole handle comes from a cut section of bicycle inner tube. Just cut a length long enough to fit from blade to pommel—brush on slippery rubber cement and slide the whole piece on. Let it dry. Trim off any excess and you'll have a much-improved grip on your knife.

To improve your grip even more, fit the handle with a sling—much the same as you fit your rifle with a sling. You can run a piece of leather from the new hole in the top or bottom of the quillion to the pommel. Slide your hand in between the sling and handle. With the sling pressed tightly against the back of your hand, you will be more secure when using your knife.

Manufacturers also like to maintain some semblance of balance, but in doing so, they are wrong. Years ago, we used to put our finger on the quillion to see which way the blade would go. Knife makers are no doubt doing the same today, but they have to stop. Blade heavy knives are for throwing, and throwing your knife away is a terrible idea.

For *Great Livin' in Grubby Times* , we got our E&E (Escape and Evasion) information from the legendary Brian Adams, an honor graduate from Army Ranger School and Army SERE (Survival, Escape, Resistance and Survival) School. He is steadfast about the necessity of maintaining control over your weapons. So are we.

You need a handle heavy knife, or, put another way, your knife has to be blade-light. Otherwise, you suffer the loss of speed and control, both of which are the keys to utility and combat victory. This maxim is especially true for a lady's knife, because she won't have enough power in her wrists to move heavy weight around quickly. That's too bad, because speed and agility are always the advantage of the lightweight people.

Besides size, consider handle shape. Finger ridges are a great idea, and some people even put in an extra finger groove.

My only taboo for handle material is metal. In temperature extremes, you won't be able to touch the handle. Also, metal conducts electricity. Spyderco recently received a letter from an electrical worker who saved a life when he cut the power line jolting his friend's almost dead body. No damage to him; Spyderco's knives' handles are apparently made of insulating material. I'm sure they don't claim this---products liability, you know. Nevertheless, they got the letter.

By now you know that a spear is much better than a knife for a lot of functions. Fishing is just one. As you will learn in the self defense chapters, a spear will keep you at a safe distance from an attacker. That includes wild bears, incidentally. So---I would like a handle that attaches easily to a pole.

Our own design of knife employs a hollow, non-magnetic stainless steel handle, and you can store LOTS of useful life-savers down inside. You can fill your handle better than your mom could fill your Christmas stocking with a can of survival goodies from MPI. In addition, I have some items of my own. Monofilament line is my favorite survival item to carry. If your survival knife doesn't have it, buy some. With low visibility, it makes snares, shelter, ridge lines for a drop cloth, tie-offs, and trip lines. It also cleans off easily and doesn't impregnate with your scent, the way cord does.

A quillion in front of a hunting knife handle is an absolute necessity. But they're often made out of shiny brass and sharp edged steel, so the first time you rely on them to protect you, they jam your hand so sharply that the resulting pain makes you lose your grip. When we say quillion, we mean a properly designed device that comfortably stops your hand from sliding onto the blade. That's why you need to file your knife's quillion. If it hurts you when your hand goes against it, it's dangerous because pain will make you lose control. A thumb rest will help you to push a dull blade through something hard.

Besides the quillion, your knife needs a good pommel on the back of the handle that provides a physical protrusion you can pull on. Without that, you rely on grip friction alone to retrieve your knife. That's another important reason to drill the pommel. You can easily fashion a thong to go around your body---thus increasing your pulling power by hundreds of pounds.

A few times, I have jammed my knife into a tree or rock crack so hard I needed to find Mr. World to retrieve it. It can happen to

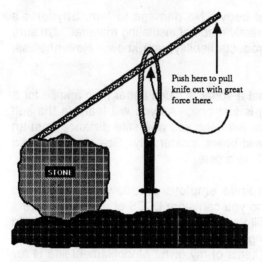

Push here to pull knife out with great force there.

STONE

you. Don't leave home without a holey pommel.

As we mentioned earlier, it is also a good idea to have a pommel hardened for pounding or chipping. It wouldn't cost that much more, and the woods utility would be substantially increased. Just a few, well placed nails in your home away from home will make a world of difference, and a hard, flattened pommel pounds them in with ease. To use your pommel for pounding, you would put a hole in the tip of the sheath to carry a wrist thong. Using the thong with your knife in the sheath would make your complete knife into a hammer.

How about a thong hole? I don't know why, but over half the knife handles I see don't provide that critically valuable addition. A thong doubles your control-ability, secures your knife with a long line to your belt, and allows you to hang your knife within easy reach (especially at night).

Knife handles just don't come out of the box with all the additions we've talked about. That's okay. You can modify most of the knife handles in the world and bring them up to your new standard of excellence.

Do that—-and your knife will work far better for you than anything on the market.

110

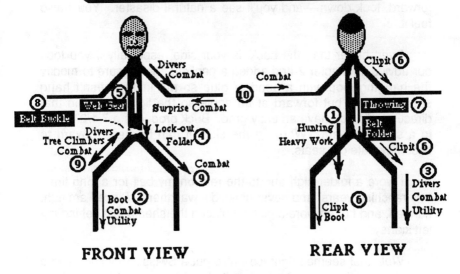

BODY MAP FOR KNIFE CARRY

Front View labels:

Divers Combat

Web Gear ⑤

⑧ Belt Buckle

Surprise Combat

Divers Tree Climbers Combat ⑨

Lock-out Folder ④

Combat ⑨

⑩

Boot ② Combat Utility

FRONT VIEW

Rear View labels:

Clip it ⑥

Combat →

Throwing ⑦

Hunting Heavy Work ①

Belt Folder

Clip it ⑥

③ Divers Combat Utility

Clip it ⑥ Boot

REAR VIEW

Chapter 10

WAYS AND MEANS TO CARRY YOUR KNIFE

Even before you attach your knife to your body, you have to wrap it in a safe container, called a sheath.

Leather used to be the thing. Not any more. I like nylon. Leather is heavy; it requires maintenance, and water isn't good for it. On the other hand, nylon can be dyed, is washable, bendable, lighter, etc. That's my choice. Heavy nylon, of course; some of the lightweight stuff will allow the blade to slip through and cut you.

The trick in carrying a knife is to feel **for** it rather than feel it. It's not supposed to make you uncomfortable. But you always want to be able to grab it when you need it.

111

A lot of how you carry your knife depends on what it will be used for. Most of us use a knife as a tool. Carrying is therefore simple; it just about always hangs on the belt.

But we are only referring to half the belt; that's the half that goes around the back. If you like looking at natural disasters, carry your knife on the front of your belt. All you have to do is bend forward, look down—and you'll see a natural disaster. You'll also feel it.

Even better than the back, is your side, especially if you took our advice in chapter 2 and added a penlight. Make sure to modify the hanging loop with a bead of glue so the knife doesn't hang straight down, but forward at an angle so the light shines in that direction and you have an easy grab. Buck produces a 7 1/2" blade in a swivel-sheath. Worn on the side, it can be bent forward to accommodate car seats.

I wore a folder high and to the rear on my belt for a long time, (my ranching years) and never noticed it was there. Since I am right handed, and I often wore a pistol, I placed the sheath just behind my left kidney.

Well, that seemed right, so I also put a Swiss Army knife and a Buck trapper (jammed into the same sheath) right next to the folder. The two stayed side by side, and I had utility very few hunters dream of. When I added a pocket steel, however, (3rd sheath) I noticed the weight, so I backed off.

If you don't want to arouse public interest, think concealment and wear a boot knife. It's a great way to carry a second knife, and it may work for you when you can't reach for your primary. A boot carry isn't the quickest. You have to reach down, pull your trousers up over your knife and then make your grab, which can take forever. Also, boot knives are notorious for pee-wee handles.

That's because a boot knife has to be flat on one side so the handle's edge doesn't dig into your leg. Another reason for a small handle is blade balance, which makes it throw better. But, knives are not for throwing. Get the point now and you won't have somebody stick you with it later.

Boot Knife. Notice the double edge. Get this knife sharp and it will provide super defense because it cuts both left and right. Note the clip on the side of the sheath---made to go on the top rim of your boot on <u>the outside</u>.

If your knife is going to be used for defense, (or war), then you can think about a more exotic way to carry it. Upside down on a field harness is common. Just make sure to tie it in with solder wire so it doesn't come out unless it's invited—-by a strong yank with your hand. For underwater, one of my knives fits on the left shoulder of my diving wetsuit, and it's retained by Velcro.

Concealment is fine, but your knife will only do some good for you when it's in your hand. If you will be in situations where you may need it fast, place it somewhere on your body within arm's reach.

Which arm? It depends on whether or not you carry superior firepower. Of course, a superior weapon (pistol) is held in your more co-ordinated hand, which means your knife will be drawn by the other.

That's why I don't like a pistol holster with a knife sheath attached. You wind up with your blaster in your right hand, and if you need your knife you have to call, "time out."

To rip your knife out in a hurry, cut open its sheath and then sew the sheath back together with weaker thread so you can yank your blade out quickly by busting through those threads. Parachutists often do this so it will be easy to draw their knife and cut lines to get themselves out of trouble. Divers do something similar with soldering wire. Use the wire to hold your knife at any angle; perhaps upside down in a sheath. The wire holds it securely, but a quick yank pulls the wire apart so you have your knife in your hand.

Push-handle knives are frequently employed as belt buckles. I just can't get enthused. The knife itself is difficult to use for slicing because human wrist flex doesn't work that way. As we said in defense, you have to over-extend dangerously to score with it. Finally, when you pull a knife on anyone un-armed, you're **wrong.** You're **even more wrong** if you get surprised and the other guy has a gun.

The way you carry your knife depends primarily on its intended use. Hopefully, all of your knives will hang from your belt, which means you don't consider yourself a knife fighter.

That's great. May your life be long and full of peace . . .

Chapter 11

THE KNIFE AS A DEFENSIVE TOOL

We wrote two separate chapters on self defense because our judicial system treats males and females differently when charged with assault. If a woman slices an attacker's hands and wrists, society shrugs its shoulders and moves forward. If a man uses a knife on somebody, however, the perp-victim goes to a hospital and the victorious citizen goes to jail.

Also, their respective combat requirements are different. Men are stronger, and they frequently get into fights where the face-off arises out of pride. On the other hand, women most often come into conflict because somebody preceives them to be a good victim. Women need to learn some simple moves and procedures to survive in a porn-infested world.

We don't expect women to engage in knife combat voluntarily. For that matter, we don't advise men to do it either, although we know some will.

But given the way crime pays in modern times, the effectiveness of our criminal justice system with early prison releases, some drug-crazed goon with a lead pipe could attack at any time. In a surprise attack, your knife may be all you have. Knives don't cost much; therefore, apply the American Express slogan, and <u>"Don't leave home without one."</u>

The idea in knife combat is not to get hurt. Above all, you don't want to go to a hospital to catch up on your Jello. Therefore, the first rule is: **Never. . . !**

NEVER GET INTO KNIFE-TO-KNIFE COMBAT.
YOU MIGHT LOSE, OR TIE

Of course, losing violates the survivors' maxim: "Better to be judged by twelve than finally judged by One." A tie in a knife fight means both parties make a blood donation to mother earth.

All of the above means you have two chances out of three of spilling your own blood.

If the other guy draws a knife on you, you can draw yours, but you'd better be telling your feet to get wings. You may be the best blocker in the world, you may know how to parry like a French swordsman, but nothing—-nothing at all prevents injury like safe distance from danger.

So, rule number two is:

KEEP OUT OF RANGE

Every so often you will see a knife with a handguard designed to be used also as brass knuckles. Like a deck gun on a submarine, it's a dumb idea. You can't use the knuckles unless you get into close range, where a decent karate man can demolish your teeth fast enough to make a dentist envious.

Never risk it and go in close. Stay away from this guy; wait for him to make the mistakes, and then counter-attack by slicing on exposed extremities. That way, your enemy can't reach you, and every time he tries, he suffers a severe loss.

Somebody with some brains has taught the Russian Special Forces the value of range, especially in a knife fight. Their Spitz/Natz carries a great knife, and when they line up to knife-fight, they push a button to spring the blade 25 meters ahead. Surprise.

In *RAIDERS OF THE LOST ARK*, Harrison Ford was faced— not by a knife—but by an expert, sword- wielding terrorist. Harrison drew his pistol and blew the problem away. Do the same if you can.

If they can't get near you, they can't hurt you. That's why we recommend that you learn to use a Bo (long wooden staff) in Book II of *Everybody's Outdoor Survival Guide.* The Bo allows you to strike your enemy from a safe distance. Even better, attach your knife to the end of the Bo. You are far better off to turn your knife into a spear. With our method, it doesn't take too much time. Any broomstick or tree limb will work. Just one good maneuver, and the fight should be over. If the pole is smooth, you simply line up on your target, and take a pool-cue shot, then retract it as fast as you shoved it out.

Above and beyond all, don't get mad. You will need to think your way through some quick combat moves with full concentration, and anger will block those thought patterns. Stay cool.

Rule number three is:

TWO HANDS FOR SURVIVORS.
If you aren't using both hands on one weapon, such as a spear, you should use a separate weapon in each hand. With only one weapon in one hand, you go into a fracas using 50% of your capability. So, you're going to be half effective. Worse, with only one weapon—a knife—in one hand, you allow your opponent the luxury of defending against only the knife. One hand empty is dumb. Two, at least, will make 'em worry.

A tonfa (side handled baton used by police) would be great, although you may not have one around. You need something easy to carry, something that you probably would have around all the time. One good idea is to convert a pair of nung chuks into a key chain. Out of the factory, "chucks" are a bear to use; you smack yourself at least a dozen times while trying to learn to smack an opponent.

With the striking stick shortened, you don't have to worry about the free-swinging end coming back at you. Put some weight on it. A lead fishing sinker for ocean bottom fishing will provide some good oomph. Hang it with the keys on the business end of the chain.

Learn to use a key chain like this, and you will set up some terrific openings for your stronger hand—the one with the knife in it.

What weapon you fill your weak hand with doesn't matter a whole lot, just make sure to use **something**. When you talk about using a knife in a self defense situation, you are talking about deadly combat; you simply cannot afford to finish second in a field of two.

Hollywood directors like to charge their movie-moments with excitement, so they always have the bad guy stab or swing wildly. If that's where you took your knife training, plan on moving near Hollywood permanently, like Forest Lawn Mortuary. Stabbing is a bad, no, a terrible idea. Why? In order to do it you have to close the range. If your opponent is similarly armed, you could easily wind up exchanging stab wounds.

Rule number four is:

KEEP YOUR BALANCE
Once off balance with a knife in your hand, you set yourself up for attack (you can't block well from an off-balance position). Forget the wild slice. You can't afford to make any lunge, side swipe, etc. which will pull you off balance when your opponent ducks, or steps neatly to the rear. You may suffer injury, and/or lose your weapon.

The most important rule of knife fighting is simple: **Don't!** If you must, remember:

KEEP OUT OF RANGE.
USE TWO HANDS.
STAY IN BALANCE.

Do all of the above, and you will live to enjoy your grandchildren.

Chapter 12

KNIVES IN WOMENS' SELF DEFENSE

Rape is a common crime in this country; one occurs every six minutes, and the record-keepers believe many are unreported. Since I originally wrote that statement, things have gotten worse. According to the 1992 *Information Please Almanac*, released rapists are 10.5 times more likely to be re-arrested for the same crime than first- time arresteds. I believe I know why this is, but I can't fix the problem. You can, however, and Path Finder hired an expert, Craig Huber, to write the *Complete Defense Manual*, due for publication in mid-1992.

Time Magazine recently reported that one in four American women will become rape victims.

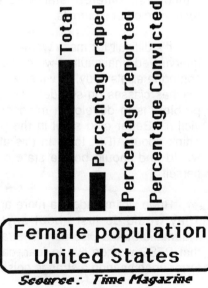

Female population
United States

Source: Time Magazine

For most of us, it's hard to comprehend the horror of the crime. I worked for a time on the Youth Crisis Hotline, where we handled 1-800-HIT-HOME hotline phone calls for help from youths 18 and under from all over the nation. Some of the calls were utterly depressing, especially those coming from raped teenagers. Even more depressing is this: They were often manipulated into believing the rape was their fault. In addition to feeling abused, filthy, and worthless, they had been brainwashed into feeling guilty. Odd as it might sound, our first order of business on the phone was to convince them they were victims.

Given the declining state of security for women, we feel it's wise to prepare. If your chances of being abused are one in four, perhaps it's time you decided against becoming a victim. Of course nobody volunters for victim; but, I want you to go a step further. Decide now, it's either you or them, and plan accordingly.

Since the nature of the crime pits a more muscular and violence-prone male against a female, you really need an edge. Double razor-edge is better. Thus, **we turn to the knife.** Knives are substantially cheaper than most handguns, and require a lot less maintenance. Besides that, handguns present a lot of travelling difficulties. Different states have different laws and they won't recognize other's permits.

It's difficult for many women to become "knife-fighters." I have interviewed unassaulted women who are squeamish about cutting someone else's body. A writer we recently hired to write on defense teaches classes on self defense for women and tells me, "the first problem is to develop a mindset. You don't have to become a victim. Better cold steel in the perpetrator's body than contact." Think about AIDS, too. In this atmosphere, I believe mortal fear would and should be the state of mind of any woman defending herself.

Rape victims adopt a more aggressive attitude after the crime. They would do just about anything to avoid PTSD, or Post-Traumatic-Stress-Disorder. The rape crisis center counselor reports that PTSD women live in fear, can't sleep nights, and wake up in terror upon hearing a strange noise. Fear imprisons them for life.

One quick piece of advice about using a knife: **Don't bluff.** Most street-wise criminals, themselves, are masters at bluffing, and they don't fool. Once your knife is out, don't even think, "scared to cut." In your mind, you must prepare to be vicious, and you have to be ready to use your knife—-with vigor.

Legalities aside, you can do just about anything, and the fine arguments about whether the force you used was excessive probably will never even be heard. Just in case you do have some kind of legal problem after an attack, however, listen to the advice of Sidney Filson, a martial arts writer for many years. With regards to the investigating police she wrote three vital words: **"Tell them nothing."**

The rape crisis center in Honolulu reports that over 50% of rapes are committed by attackers who are under alcoholic influence, so you can't rely very much on any humane inhibitions. That's one reason the old advice on submitting is being changed. In a rape situation, you will be dealing with some rough characters. An aggressive defense is better. Just don't make any stabbing maneuvers unless you have a clear unobstructed opening; they're too risky. Keep your distance and use the move we teach you. Also, carry more than one knife. A *Clipit* in the side of your shoe or boot would allow you to draw your knees up if you were flat on the ground and get your hands on a great weapon.

We are going to teach you to preserve your integrity and sanity, but you have to face the issue. The time to prepare mentally is now; we can't do that for you. Decide now that you will set aside fear and act according to plan. Once your mind is made up, buy the knife you need as well as a toy rubber knife, and begin practice.

Your knife defense will work with one simple maneuver: Flick your wrist.

To do this most effectively, you need a double-edged knife with a razor-sharp (on both sides) blade. On a folder, or switch-blade, the back side of the blade is exposed, and therefore dangerous to carry. For ladies' defense, we like the *Clipit* because it carries so you can easily get to it, opens with one hand, and **cuts very well.**

If you use a sheathed, double-edged knife, pay a few dollars and have your knife sharpened on both sides professionally. You will be amazed at the difference. The thing will cut like you wouldn't believe, and if it's stainless, it will stay sharp forever. Then, toss it in your purse and forget it—unless you board a plane.

As we talk to victims of various crimes, we find out they became members of that class because they were surprised. Most often, they didn't see it coming. But then, when we further got into the story, we learned that they didn't want to see it coming. Many didn't see it because fear blocked out their perceptions completely. No matter what the reason for failure to see the danger, you must prepare yourself.

Prepare. That doesn't mean wait 'til you're in a rainstorm and then look around for an umbrella. You have to get ready before you go out in the rain. With defense, you must think your way through and make up your mind. Here's how. Simply adopt a DefCon philosophy. DefCon is short for **Def**ense **Con**dition. Use three stages:
1. Suspicion only. No real cause to believe anything might be wrong, you just think there **might** be.
2. Suspicion only, but the suspected danger is too close to you. You feel fear.
3. Real cause to believe you're in immediate danger, coupled with fear.

How to handle yourself in DefCon 1. First, **don't ignore the problem.** Many perpetrators are egged on when they perceive an attitude of fear and helplessness. They are total cowards, and bullying is their way of compensating for the smallness they live with. If your intuitions are right, this situation will develop to #2, and DefCon #3 is sure to follow when you ignore the problem. Whatever you are occupied with, a bag of groceries, a child, gets secondary attention. Go on alert. Get your weapons into your hands. Load the chamber of a firearm. Prepare to shoot your mace. Open knives. Slip your hand through the wrist loop in the same way you would if you were playing racquet ball. The wrist loop is important because you don't want your knife to be taken away from you or knocked out of your hand. Hold your weapons down out of sight until the danger has passed. You can try to get ready on the sly, but don't worry about someone seeing you with a knife, or mace can. If they aren't looking to harm you, you will put them on alert and they'll steer clear. **Confront the danger** both physically and mentally. Speak to the person approaching you or who is blocking your way. Think about attacking (you want your attitude to be a bit pushy) and say something on the order of, "Excuse me. You're blocking my way and I'd like you to move." Do <u>not</u> look away.

DefCon #2. Weapons ready to go. Stare down your attacker. Speak with an angry, resentful voice and say something like, "You're not responding to my instructions to move out of my way. You're putting me in mortal fear, which is a valid legal reason to kill you." **Don't bluff.** Long before this confrontation, you should have figured out the answer to the famous question posed by Sean Connery to Kevin Kostner in *The Untouchables,* "What are you prepared to do?"   Do you want to be judged by twelve or carried out by six? Once you have your mind set, don't waver. A sign of weakness only invites attack.

DefCon 3. Read Rick Woodcroft, a Special Forces medic with a black belt in Judo, who wrote on self defense in *Everybody's Survival Guide.* When it's time to fight, let fly with all you got. You will never win a war by playing defense. This situation calls for you

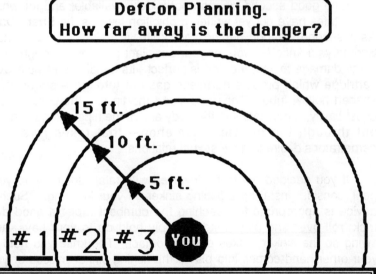

DefCon Planning.
How far away is the danger?

15 ft.

10 ft.

5 ft.

#1 #2 #3 You

A big factor in danger is range. Anything suspicious within 15 ft. from you calls for DefCon #1 precautions. If you don't go to DefCon #1 several times a year, you're not properly prepared.

to go on offense with everything you have. Attack viciously, without remorse or mercy. Follow through. Destroy your enemy.

Fake it; be coy. Pretend to give up. Act submissive. Then fire, spray, cut, or whallop. Keep on. Then keep on keeping on. Don't leave any room for this perpetrator to get up and get even. A wounded male ego can kill you and enjoy it.

YOUR SECOND WEAPON
Besides your knife, you should have some kind of weapon in your free hand. Women in Hawaii can't carry mace legally, so I bought a yiwara stick key chain for my daughter. It's really nothing more than one half a nung-chuk.

The choice of any weapon is dictated by: range and lethality. Extending your attack range means you don't have to let the perpetrator get close to you. Guns keep your perpetrator farthest away. Mace let's him in as close as 15 ft. A knife or club operates almost on contact. Guns and knives can be lethal, clubs and mace are merely deterrents.

One good second weapon not widely available, and for which most states have not yet written prohibition laws, is the **Shark Dart.** As a second weapon behind your knife, it makes a lot of sense. Should your knife fail you, or your assailant get close enough to do some damage to you, the dart is perfect. Its handle contains a CO_2 cartridge which propels harmless gas out through a strong dart-shaped hollow tube. Once you insert the tip into the perpetrator's chest cavity, (anywhere into the body above the hips) the gas shoots out through the needle. Somehow---that takes away the perpetrator's desire to have sexual relations.

If you decided not to be involved with fatal solutions to your peril, consider installing a fishing sinker on your key ring. Such a device is appropriate for teaching the dumbest rapist a good dog trick: roll over and play dead. Simply hold on to your keys, and swing so the sinker makes cranial contact. The knife you hold in your other hand comes into play if the fishing sinker misses or you don't make solid enough contact. This thing won't do any lethal damage, so hit and run. Distance is your best defense and hiding will make someone spend hours looking for you.

Once you've decided what weapons to carry, plan your attack around your weaponry. It may happen, however, that you get caught unprepared. Most often, rape is a method of vengeance in which you, personally, are abused to "right" some wrongs in the assailant's history. Crying, begging or submitting gratifies the attacker psychologically. On the other hand, angrily screaming at the assailant may reverse the psychology of the rape. So shout, scream, insult, and while all this goes on, keep your distance.

If you do have your double-edged knife, however, take up a half sideways stance and put most of your weight on the rear leg. Crouch slightly to make sure you're well balanced. Bare feet are better than high heels unless you know how to snap a side kick. If you remove high heeled shoes and you don't have a second weapon, keep one in your free hand for use as an additional attack device.

Hold your knife hand extended toward your attacker in such a manner that you can move it easily from left to right and back again——quickly. The blade points upwards.

If your attacker sees the knife and presses on, make your bluff good. Almost always, his hands will reach toward you. As soon as he does this, you slash——quickly, in a slightly downward left and right, back-and-forth flick, cutting first the hand closest to you, then the other. **Don't** move in; wait for him to try and grab.

This is a good time to tell you that your assailant may have a knife also. Make a decision now. Either be prepared to give up, or be mentally prepared to cut him as severely as he cuts you. Most victims believe that "cut" is better than "raped." Just try to keep your distance, though. If you block his knife hand with your purse and slash with your knife, you'll have an advantage.

Not that this is a game in which we issue a score, but——a slice across his knuckles or fingers earns a 1. If you slice the inside of the hand or fingers, you get a 3 because you will probably cut tendons and the perp won't be able to make a fist or grab you. If you slash the inside wrist, you get a 7. Finally, if your blade happens to slice where he takes his pulse, you get a 10, and the attack is probably over.

*unscrew
cap here*

We think it would be a great idea to install a mace gas cannister in a hollow handle. It would spray several feet out and probably convince a jury that mortal fear was reasonable after your stabbed victim kept on coming toward you.

While this is going on, you need to be shouting and screaming. Harsh and loud noises you can make with your mouth help you in several ways. You may attract enough attention to summon someone's help. You'll startle your opponent. Most important, however, is that screaming keeps you in the proper fighting mood. You'll do a lot better with an attitude. Do not, **don't** exude fear. A display of anger always helps. That's why you keep screaming.

You need short, very quick, crafty flicks of the wrist. Let the razor edge do it's work; you don't need force. Make sure that you don't swing with your arm or indicate with any body movement when your attack will come. The movement surprises from a sudden flick of the wrist in both directions. Slice and keep on slicing until he breaks off the attack.

Don't fall down. Stay upright, and even if you are knocked down, get up and come back screaming and fighting.

Practice with a rubber knife. I believe every producer of combat knives should sell a rubber replica for practice along with a wrist weight to develop the knife owner's muscular ability to handle the real knife. You need to be confident that this works, and you need to learn how to slash with the knife across an attacker's arm. Join a personal defense class (for a few months, at least). You don't need to learn the fancy moves, but you do need the confidence.

Carry your knife and other weapons everywhere. Then, with one simple defense move, you have a great chance of staying free of attack.

Chapter 13

HOW TO TEACH
KIDS ABOUT KNIVES

In a campground once, I heard, "Johnny, don't you ever touch this knife again. A knife will cut you and make you bleed." Another father I know gave his four-year-old son a small folding lockout knife and let him play with it. Sure enough, the kid cut himself.

You may not approve of the instruction, but, both parents tried to teach something. Knowledge about knives needs to be taught in the home. When do you start? Depending on a child's maturity and ability to understand, a good time is around age 5. I begin by teaching the difference between sharp and dull.

I wait until we eat something that requires cutting, (steak) and I put two knives on the table. I show the child how to cut, and we begin with a dull knife. Then we switch to a sharp knife. Immediately he learns the difference. The rest of the lesson teaches him that a sharp knife will cut his finger or arm as easily as it cuts the meat.

I believe that giving your kids a knife is a way of telling them that benefits and responsibility always go hand-in-hand. The benefit is knife ownership; the responsibility is knife respect and safety.

To begin, I buy a cheap knife at a swap meet or garage sale. It will receive some hard use, and the edge of the blade is sure to come back customized after the child learns that it won't cut through concrete.

I prefer a Swiss Army Knife—an imitation can be had for under $10. About every third day, I introduce a new blade to the child and provide hands-on practice so that he gets an idea how it works. I start with the screwdriver blades, both flat and phillips, then teach the leather hole punch blade and scissors. Be careful with the leather hole punch; it's easy for the blade to collapse on fingers.

127

Once the little person understands what sharp is and develops some fear of cutting himself, it's time to whittle. Choose a softer wood to minimize the danger of a slip.

With the stick in one hand and knife in the other, he learns to cut away from—-not toward—-his body. When he becomes accomplished enough, I teach him how to put a point on a stick. This is the basis for his first outdoor cooking lesson. A sharpened green stick with the bark removed will holds hot dogs, then marshmallows.

I then teach how to put an edge on a stick so that it cuts grass. Again, the child learns the concepts of dull and sharp. An unsharpened stick won't cut the grass down, but a sharp stick slices right on through with a flick of the wrist.

One of the all-time favorite things children love to do is imitate what they see on TV. If it's a dumb thing for an adult to throw a knife, it's even dumber to allow a child to play this way. I give careful instructions about not throwing knives, and thus insure that the child doesn't develop a terrible habit.

<u>CAUTIONS</u>
When a child learns that a knife is not for cutting himself, he should also learn that the point is very dangerous. Show him how the point can go right into anything, and make sure he learns not to let the point get anywhere near his face.

DON'T let the child move with the blade exposed. Make sure that the blade is secure (folded into the handle or sheathed) before he takes a step. Otherwise, a running child could trip and impale himself.

Whether a child grows up in the city or in the country, knife knowledge is valuable. Teach your child to respect the tool, not only for the damage it might do, but also for the benefits it will provide. That lesson will be a valuable step toward becoming a responsible adult.

Chapter 14

A NEW DESIGN FOR A SURVIVAL KNIFE

THE PAKA
Pivot Action Knife Axe
copyright ©1984by Don Paul

In all my travels, I've never seen the ultimate survival tool. That's probably because our age-old concept of "knife" limits our thinking.

FORM FOLLOWS FUNCTION is a maxim of design. So to get a greater-than-knife-result, you need to think beyond the functions of "knife." You don't need to be a metal worker; you need to be a user and experience the limitations inherent in just the plain tool. Only when you need to do something and your knife can't perform—-do you learn how it OUGHT to work. Even if the tool is perhaps well crafted, it will be limited in usefulness—because that's all it is, just a knife.

The problem I've found in numerous jungles, mountains and Oregon's coastal rain forests is this: though many knife manufacturers have their metals together, they don't understand what an outdoor knife should or could do, so the designs, as they stand now, are lacking.

Specialty knife makers have solved some of the problems however. With he advent recently of new steels and new heat treatments, factories such as Black Jack and Cold Steel have produced edges that seem to stay sharp forever, require little maintenance, and never break.

You need a knife that functions for hunting, fishing, camping, trapping, fighting, and building. It should convert to a chopping instrument, a pole spear, a hammer, a chipper, a saw for wood or bone, a skinner, a digger, and a long range hand-to-hand defense weapon—just to name a few. If you want to discover obvious defects in equipment design, just try using the stuff at night. Most outdoor equipment manufacturers---guns, knives, packs---work by day, test by day, and go home at night. Maybe that's why they never think of the guy in the middle of the woods after dark. **Design** of the knife should not only follow these functions, but allow it to adapt to the critical skills involved in staying alive in the woods.

When I first wrote the book, no survival knife existed which would do everything that needed doing. A few came close. Today, specialty knife makers are producing top quality stuff. For a hollow handle survival knife, the Chris Reeve is hot. The whole knife is made from one piece of steel; therefore, it's strong. The enclosed plans and description have now become an instruction too. You'll find a lot of our early design features incorporated into commercial blades. If you make your own knife, all our features don't have to be included in the manufacture; that's not a requirement of our copyright. If you need to cut cost, cut out some of the more difficult details. When your knife-maker is finished, however, you will own the very best, custom, knife, and it should last you for life.

Start with THE SHEATH. It should hold the knife securely with nylon straps and Velcro fasteners. The handle end of the sheath will either detach or bend down toward the tip to allow unobstructed use of the hammer-chipper. Big blade sheaths need to swivel so you can sit in a truck with them strapped to your belt.

The sheath should attach to several places on the body. Note that the sheath in the drawing has lines drawn both longitudinally and across so that the knife can be worn in a variety of locations. With the 13" blade model, it will be blade-heavy and therefore could be worn on the back like an arrow-quiver. Frank Vought makes a sheath out of ABS which he calls his "mode three." That's because it attaches to the body in three different ways. Well, why not make a mode seven? A spring loaded snap (at the choil) on the inside of the sheath can hold the knife upside down in case a fast-draw is needed. We use nylon straps with Velcro for ease and speed, and they also make outside upper arm and lower leg carries possible. The knife can be inverted over a shoulder, and perhaps, concealed.

Leather is a poor choice for a survival sheath. Black nylon is better and cheaper. The sheath is open at the tip end of the knife (it's a bear to clean a sheath if it is closed-ended and dirt falls into it). Also, you want to ventilate the sheath. Air needs to circulate around the blade. Add a penlight, a small L.E.D. clock, and, of course, a compass.

Sew on a few extra pockets. One commercial sheath now manufactured overseas includes a pocket filled with a cheap, Hong Kong police whistle. Something is better than nothing; if you have the space, use it. AVID outdoor makes a first aid kit. Take a few items from that and attach the kit to your sheath on the outside.

Think about extra attachments for the sheath, such as a screw driver blade, sharpened hole for wire cutting, (pivoted against the swedge). The sheath needs to contain a diamond or ceramic rod sharpener. Some solid denim material impregnated with knifemaker's green would allow you to use the sheet for stropping.

THE KNIFE should be large—say 12" inches overall. In the drawing, we made it 13.5 inches, but the size of the blade doesn't matter—-utility does. It should weigh under a pound, dry. (dry=without handle-packed equipment). The blade should be parkerized, not shiny steel, except for the polished blood groove that will be used for a signal mirror. Drill through the center (deepest part) of that blood groove with a 1/32" bit to make a tiny hole you can sight through to send signals. Of course, drill before heat treatment.

The handle will be **hollow**, and custom-built to fit your hand. Fit it by wrapping the handle with tape, and the tape can be removed later to build or repair many useful survival gadgets—from traps to animal drags to packboards.

When making a spear from a pole cut in the woods, leave a (right angle is best) limb attached on the knife-less (free) end. You can stand on it and anchor it quickly to impale a charging animal.

That hook also will do wonders for you in hand-to-hand combat. You can sweep both legs out from under an oponnent with a butt-stroke leg sweep. Somehow, when they land hard on the ground, you get their attention.

Tapes for the handle will be in various colors, including forest green and iridescent orange. Forest green covers up shiny objects so you don't advertise your presence in the forest. A small piece of iridescent tape can be used on the back of a cap and light-charged to make you visible at night. Electrical tape is included, as is a rough grip-tite for the outer layer. Parachute cord under the last, outer layer of tape provides additional twist grip capability. It will also save your bacon when used as rope or trip lines.

The handle incorporates a corrugated hammer and a chipper. The hammer head is swung with the sheath over the knife (for safety) and can be used with the pivot handle, which fits through both blade and sheath. Thus, with a supply of nails, you could erect a quick and sturdy shelter. The chipper side can be either clawed or solid. Once shaped, heat treat it so it's hard enough to make sharp stones, arrow heads, or spear points. The hammer head end has an inside receptacle for a compass, which will read in degrees. If you can shoot a vearing (direction) with your compass and walk in that direction, you can find your way back to a given starting point (see *Never Get Lost*).

Both the tip of the knife and the end of the handle will be drilled to accept a pivot, and the pivot handle will fit into the knife handle's cavity. The pivot handle has raised ends, and will be wrapped with several lengths of monofilament line. If you don't install a pivot handle, use the knife like a MachAx with your knuckles on top of the handle and the blade **never in line** with your body.

With pivot, the knife becomes an axe for chopping or a hammer or rock chipper with the pivot through the tip and sheath. The pivot provides a long swing and multiplies the impact speed, so it hits hard and effectively from either end. Don't miss the target and kneel down on one knee to keep the blade from coming back on you.

Another use of the knife-tip hole will allow two knives to join together and make branch loppers. (Note the grind of the swedge, as shown on the drawing.)

THE BLADE. The tip sweeps up slightly to give a good, hollow ground, skinning edge. Forward of the fulcrum and pivot hole, the swedge is side sharpened, as detailed. A gut hook will open big game for dressing without nicking entrails and tainting meat.

The PAKA has to be pointed for penetration, (spear and knife), and grooved for easy withdrawal. Note the crown on the top of the blade—-it holds soldered carbide teeth for cutting metal.

The quillion is made of molded black plastic, and incorporates a bottle opener. It's drilled on the top; you sight through that hole and frame the knife tip so that the plumb line indicates all the critical heights, distances, and times we taught in Chapter 1.

The side of the hilt will protrude a half inch or so and cup to the rear to catch a pole and keep the knife from slipping backward when used in the spear mode. See the drawing at E.

DRAWING REFERENCES AND EXPLANATIONS
FOR THE KNIFE-MAKER

A.   At two locations, the knife is drilled to accept a shaft which attaches to a handle. On the tip end, the hole in the sheath matches the hole in the knife, and enables the user to pivot the knife on the handle end for pounding and chipping. On the butt-end, the pivot enables the user to hack with the knife and thus use it as an axe. Also, and again on the tip end, putting two knives together with a bolt will turn the pair of them into shears for cutting wooden limbs or wire if necessary.

B.   From the arrow forward to the tip as shown, the swedge is ground according to the detail, so that when two knives are put together, they will act as limb-loppers.

C.   Surface corrugated on the face of the hammer. Fits a standard triangular file, as does the gut hook located at G.

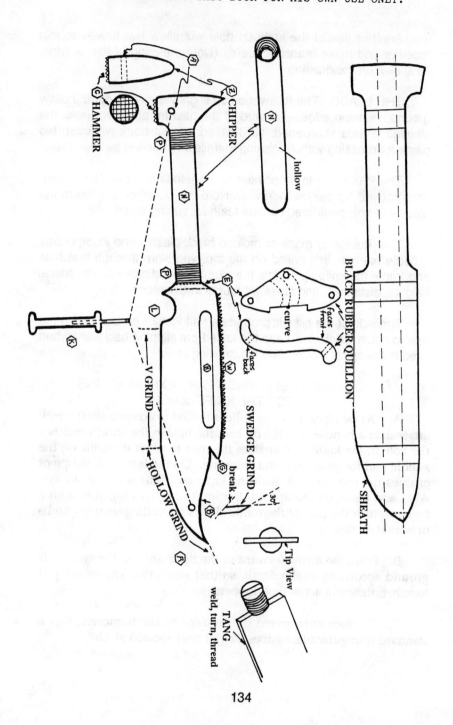

134

N.   Hollow stainless handle with fine thread on each end to match the threads on the built up tang and on the hammer head. This handle will be built up with parachute cord and various kinds and colors of tape. The final layer will be a grip tight tape to give the user a slip-free surface.

W.   A most important feature, NOT DRAWN, is the saw on the back of the knife. Note well that this surface is crowned, rather than straight. It should be ground to accept carbide tips with silver solder.

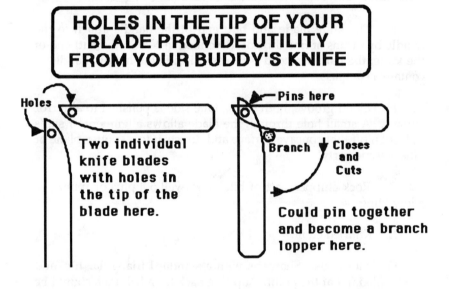

HOLES IN THE TIP OF YOUR BLADE PROVIDE UTILITY FROM YOUR BUDDY'S KNIFE

Holes

Two individual knife blades with holes in the tip of the blade here.

Pins here

Branch   Closes and Cuts

Could pin together and become a branch lopper here.

If you're ordering a custom knife with a friend, put a hole in the tip of the blade and the sheath.   Thus, you can pin your two knives together and use them for branch loppers and barbed wire cutters at the tip.   You can also pin through the blade and the sheath, then pound with the pommel.

This will be a twelve point saw with a wide set. Teeth surfaces are angled at 55 degrees. The set of the teeth must be wider than the knife to prohibit blade binding if the user cuts into the compression side of a limb or log. Since four inches of teeth ride on tip, maximum cutable limb width will be about seven inches.

E.   Black rubber quillion. Rear view, (upper left) shows how this extends to the side to catch a pole so that when the knife is attached, the user has a strong push point.   Note the holes.   This piece is extruded with a center line, and glues together over the tang just forward of the built-up (welded) threaded portion receiving the handle. Small male and female dowlings will aid fit and strength. An interchangeable blade or prybar would screw into the handle the same way.

P.   The knife blade and butt end of the handle attach to the handle by means of fine threads, described in N. On the butt end of the knife, the hammer head is recessed inside the hollow handle to contain a compass.

H.   Blood groove, both sides.   One side is polished to a mirror surface.   A small hole through the blade allows alignment of sun's reflection off that concave surface and directs it to a spotter plane or other rescue party.

Z.   Rock chipper part of hilt.   Rockwell 50, plus or minus, to allow filing.

L.   Knurled choil.

G.   Gut hook.   Sharpens with a standard triangular file, and can be filed flat at the point.   Top side back for a half inch should be dull and flat, to allow gutting without cutting an animal's peritoneum.

K.   Pivot handle.   Threaded shaft fits both tip and butt.   Wing nut fixed on shaft at handle end compresses against acorn nut, which attaches on end of shaft. Shaft swings against stop on inside of handle to allow only 120 degrees of swing.   Inset section on handle between raised edges allows for wrapping with monofilament fish line, which then covers with non-slip tape. Handle length conforms to allowable storage space inside knife handle tube.   Inside of pivot handle is also hollow, to allow for additional storage.

Chapter 15

HOW TO BUY A KNIFE

Basically, you have five ways to go. You can buy new or used. If you buy new, you have a choice of foreign or domestic. You can make your own. Finally, you can have one custom-made for you.

Either buy American or buy from an American knife parts importer. That's not a patriotic statement. I tell you that purely based on my responsibility to get you, my reader, the best deal. Since we suffer so much in this country with governmental interference, manufacturers are hard put to the task of competing with foreign nations. Add a little labor demand to the problem, and competition is near impossible. So cars, electronics, etc. are better imported. I think knives may be the exception, however. As I look around, it's hard to beat the American products.

USED

My own knife collection includes a bunch of used knives, purchased primarily because I have to experiment. I paid $7 in a secondhand shop for a good Gerber knife originally costing about $30. On another occasion, I paid half a dollar for a broken fillet knife from Brunton; the wood handle is beautiful. Second hand knives are frequently found at swap meets or flea markets, garage sales and second hand stores. By now you have an idea of the shape blade you would like, and maybe you even know what kinds of knives (lock-out folder, sheath, etc) you would like to use in the field.

Don't worry about how dull the knife is. Most good second hand knives are discarded by people who don't know how to sharpen, or where to have it done for them. If the knife is dull, so much the better. Probably, the lack of cutting edge was the primary reason for the owner's getting rid of it. With a diamond sharpener and this book, you'll put the blade back in great shape quickly.

What spells disaster in a used knife is discoloration on the blade. The change in color means that part of the knife was overheated, which normally occurs from excessive grinding on the blade's edge. So it lost its temper in the discolored area, was overhardened where the discoloration stops, and will probably break right at that place sometime in the future. Forget it.

Also, I'm not too big on rust. If a new knife is rusty, that means the cutting edge is pitted. You can take a file and some stones to it, but it **will rust** again. Metal coatings and platings only hide what's going on at the cutting edge, where the naked eye can't see it.

The handle can be a mess, especially if you know how to fix it. Modern glues are wonderful for healing breaks in bone or plastic finishes. Several knife parts and accessories vendors advertise in *Knife World* and *Blade Magazine.* For the sheath knife, we recommend taping or plastic wood to get a good handle-to-hand fit anyway, so don't let the handle throw you.

You may find a knife with a broken blade. Don't let that stop you. If you're careful to keep the blade cool, you can grind it back into a (shorter, of course) useful cutter. Just pay accordingly. People who use cheaper production knives for prybars shouldn't have a lot of money handed to them for selling the broken results of their folly.

Buying a used knife can provide you with an early production model from a large, well-known manufacturer who paid closer attention to quality control in the early stages of company growth.

However, with knives, the old saying, "They don't make 'em like they used to," isn't true. In fact, "They make 'em better." New steels, new innovations, and some acquired experience have made today's knives better than ever. In the 50's and 60's, you would find hot rodders designing innovations for their cars which made a lot of sense. A few years later, you would see the same innovation being discovered by a production model giant. The case with knives is much the same.

Lynn Thompson of Cold Steel was proud of telling me, "We were the first to use Kraton; now everybody uses it." That was only an indication of their super quality. Mike Stewart, owner of Blackjack knives tells me, "I have discovered the secrets of cross sectional geometry and heat treatment." Try his Mamba model; the blade and knife design are simply incredible. Jerry Younkins tested Blackjack's knives for us and results were amazing. Thus, if you have the money, think about buying a new knife. If you can, pay 15% to 25% more for a specialty blade. You get back 200% in performance and edge retention.

NEW FOREIGN
Think your way through this maze thusly: New World countries, such as Japan, Germany, make good stuff, but I am convinced we are better at metalurgy and heat treatment, so the better blades are from the USA. I wish our economy was quality controlled by knifesmiths, but it ain't. Because foreign dollars are stronger than ours, their products cost a lot of (our) money.

I won a ($28) Puma White Hunter shooting skeet in Germany in 1966, and used the knife until a burglary 10 years later. Today, that same model costs over $100. Many new foreign knives cost more than a comparable U.S. product. From a real Third World country, you can get a cheapo price, but, the knife is junk. You are much better off with a used American knife than you are with a similarly priced new Third World product.

The exception to the rule would probably come from a good knife importers such as SOG or Taylor Cutlery. SOG imports from Japan, and Taylor frequently builds his products with parts from as many as five different countries. Thus, you get an inexpensive knife. that will often do a decent job. What's the bottom line? Good foreign quality won't be as good as U.S. good quality and will often cost a lot more. Since the key to surviving any emergency frequently depends on tool quality, forget the Third World junk.

NEW U.S.A.
Take a close look at Blackjack's Mamba or Cold Steel's Trailmaster. (See the picture pages, back of this book.) As Crocodile Dundee said in a New York subway, "Now, that's a knyfe!" Both took hair off my arm right out of the box, and they chop 2 X 4's all day long, but still retain their sharpness. That's durability.

139

With American knife makers, you pretty much get what you pay for. Competition keeps individual manufacturers from price gouging. So, any American knife you buy will most likely be price worthy. Thus, the choice breaks down to the kinds of knives you should have for your personal use, and the shape of blade that will perform for you best.

Granted, the manufacturers in this country are slow to innovate. You would be also, if you thought some lawyer would crawl out of the woodwork and sue you. But with the changes we gave you in the early chapters of this book, you can make an American product much more useful.

CUSTOM

Got big bucks? I was really taken with the beauty of some of the custom knives I saw, so I wrote to inquire about the price. Answer: $750. Jerry Younkins disagrees with me when I say custom knives are too expensive. One example he cites is Frank Vought, owner of Outfitter Knives, 115 Monticello Dr. Hammond, Louisiana, 70401. (call 504-345-0278, but watch the time from outside USA). You can get a catalog for $2. Frank makes almost all of his knives with ATS-34 steel, which is the latest and greatest according to Jerry. His average waiting period for a custom order is 6-8 weeks, and his prices are competitive because he deals direct. He uses Kydex, a smooth ABS formula material, for sheaths. One such sheath is his "mode-3" which can be carried upright, in a boot, or inverted.

Pricing is most often higher for customs simply because it takes more time for one man to make a single knife than for a factory to make many. Still, you may have some ideas of your own, especially now that you have this book. If you want your knives to look better, perform better, or be unique, custom is the way to go.

Finally, you can make your own knife. Since we are talking only about some grinding and some handle fabrication, I recommend you try to make at least one. We teach how in the next chapter.

Chapter 16

HOW TO MAKE A KNIFE

Who in the world wants to make a knife when they can often buy a good used one for under $10? You do! Are you one of these cooks who make biscuits and cakes from a mix out of a box or are you a scratch cook? Either way, you can produce a great knife. They make mixes in a kit for you---all you have to do is shake and bake (actually glue, rivet and perhaps solder). Besides that, this chapter will teach you the basics on cooking up a knife from scratch.

It's not that you need the knife. You need the experience. If you've read our *GREEN BERETS' GUIDE TO OUTDOOR SURVIVAL* series, you know that things may collapse entirely, and you may find yourself short of good tools and implements. You may also run out of ammunition and find your supply shut off at the main gate. That's why we decided to publish *Ammo Forever.*

The most important implement for survival you will ever need is a knife. Thus, it's a good idea to learn how to make a blade, a handle, perhaps a guard or quillion to separate the two, and a sheatht. Thus, it isn't the blade you're after, it's the training.

However, you may want a deal on a great knife you knocked together yourself. With no products liability insurance to pay, no government interference in your shop, no EEOC to contend with, you can get a first class knife for half price. Enter Jantz 1-800-351-3082 Supply, who will sell you a fine 440-C stainless blade with a full tang, plus the handle and fasteners---often for under $20. For a five dollar bill, they will send you a catalog and a project booklet.

I'm enthused. Jantz reports that many of their buyers double their money on Jantz kits after they put the knives together and take them to a show. Of course, a knife will sell better if it comes with a sheath. Therefore, I plan to take my little Spanish speaking cuerpo South and try to find a cheap leather sheath. Ethan Becker tells me sheaths cost almost what the knife does. If I can get a deal, I'll make up patterns and ship quantity to Jantz.

Perhaps, you spend some of your earthly time wandering through junkyards, garage sales and secondhand stores. Some good sources of blades are:
> The steel from an auto's leaf spring.
> Any industrial file.
> A keyhole saw.
> A hacksaw.

You will need a carborundum grinding wheel and lots of water to shape the blade. Make sure to **grind slowly** as you apply blade to wheel. **Don't allow the metal to overheat.** You can't afford to lose the temper built into your piece of steel when it was originally heat treated. Move the knife across the wheel so that one spot on the blade never gets a chance to heat up. Also, be more careful when grinding near the point, where you don't have a lot of backup metal to which heat can transfer.

Working with the piece of future knife blade you've found, (the steel blank) outline a pattern on some kind of paper (perhaps cardboard). Think about how you want your knife to perform and apply our blade shape principles. An auto spring will make a good (beefy) center-point knife. Wide, flat files are great for building blades with arched skinning surfaces. From old key-hole saw blades, you may be thinking about a long-bladed fillet knife. Hacksaw blades become small skinners for squirrels and rabbits.

Trace one side out on your blank, then slip the outline over to the other side and trace it out again. When you're sure both sides of your layout are the same, you can start grinding. Go easy when grinding. Keep the metal wet always, and remove it from the wheel as soon as you see the water evaporating. Remember, you have to grind both ends of the knife. Shaping the blade takes time and patience. Without patience, you'll over heat the metal.

Consider the heavy weight of a big knife, and shape the handle-end down to a tang to be covered later with some kind of handle material. On the other hand, blades for fine cutting can be full size, that is, the tang's side edges can show after they are sandwiched in between handle material.

With the whole knife shaped and somewhat sharpened, fix your attention on something to hold the knife with, called a handle. In its most simple form, it can be a lot of tape around the handle end of the blade. Other handles are made from nice looking pieces of wood, such as stag horns off a deer, or plastic wood. Jantz ships their kits with Micarta handles, so their knives take on the look of something you would buy in a mall.

This last choice is an excellent one, because it can be molded to fit your hand. What good is a knife you can't hold on to? Not much. Also, think about cork or lightweight wood on a fillet knife. It's a good idea to make it so it floats. Most of the Jantz knives have holes drilled in the tang. When you make your own from scratch, drill a hole in the tang. On a fish fillet knife, attach a float.

Form fit the inside of the handle to the tang of the knife. Simply lay the tang against the half shell, trace it out, and frind away the excess material so the tang fits in the handle, which in turn fits your hand. Before closing the handle over the tang, wax it down (or oil it) to keep it from rusting.

You get more stength in your knife with a full tang. Also, full tangs give you more support for handle attachment. Finally, the balance of the knife is better for use, because the weight in the handle comes closer to the weight of the blade.

If you use a full handle (edges showing like sandwich meat) you can put the whole thing together with rivets. Simple drill through the whole mess, and flatten the rivets out. Note that the sides of your tang consist of softer metal and therefore easier to inscribe with I.D.

Lots of glues on the market today will cause two pieces of handle to stick to your new tang. In addition, wrap the handle with tapes. If you can obtain the kind of sticky rubber used for opening jars, cut it into strips and affix (glue) it to the handle's sides.

After you install a handle on your knife, you can sharpen it just as you would any other. Push down hard on progressively harder stones, or use easy-lapping diamonds if you're in a hurry. Since this is not 440-C stainless, the knife will rust unless you keep it oiled.

You just have to carry your knife in something. Otherwise it cuts everything from furniture to car seats. If your sheath doesn't encase your knife blade well, the knife acts something like a bank teller, and inscribes notes on your personal cheeks.

If you can find some heavy nylon, use it. Most likely however, you'll be stuck with the old standby, cowhide. That's not the best choice because tannic acid will attack and discolor your blade.

Just as with the shape of the blade, the design of the sheath centers around use. If you'll be trudging through the coastal mountain ranges where the growth is thick and always wet, a long sheath will gather a lot of garbage. The best design covers only the blade. Just make sure to design the sheath with a retaining strap. That's one big reason why a quillion should be incorporated into the knife design; the strap of the sheath goes over the quillion to hold the knife in place.

Wrap your piece of leather around the blade with the folded edge around the back, not the sharp side, of your blade. Rivets are better than stitching. They are faster to install and more sturdy around the sharp edge of the blade. Attach a large belt loop to the main body of the sheath, and modify it as we taught earlier so you marry the belt to the loop. Once married, the knife stays home where it belongs.

Without a knife, your chances of survival are much slimmer. Once you've ground a couple of blades and put handles on them however, you'll know you can stay alive and well anywhere.

GLOSSARY

Aitch bone. Cartilage separating the two halves of the pelvis, or hip bone. Cuts easy on a young animal; older bones require a hatchet.

Barbless hook. Some bureaucrat's idea of keeping fish in California Lakes. It doesn't have the little sticker-point on it going in the opposite direction, so fish can wriggle off. It works well for sewing up a heavy laceration wound.

Blade and Handle. If you don't know what these are, give this book back and forget it.

Choil. The curved, unsharpened half finger hole next to the quillion on the edged side of the blade.

Clinometer. A device used to measure the angular incline of a hill or ramp. Ours is different, inasmuch as the measured angle doesn't matter if the proper trig function is applied.

Clip. That part of the backside of the blade that bends or angles down from the straight part—forward to the point.

Declinate. To measure the angle between magnetic North and True North, then to apply that data to your map for navigation purposes. You're far better off to use a navigation system that doesn't require this tedious and often error-filled process. (Try _Never Get Lost_, Path Finder 9.95)

Declination. We hate it, (and took it completely out of our own land navigation system.) But sometimes, it's useful if you want to co-ordinate the true north on a map with the magnetic north from your compass. It's the difference, in degrees, between the geographic north pole and the magnetic spot miles away to which compasses are attracted.

Dusk. Our definition. The time during which you still have workable daylight, but no sunlight.

Inertia. Whack. Clout. The smack of a blow. In college talk, it's the product of mass times velocity. If you want to hit something harder, either hit it faster or increase the weight behind the blow.

145

Nung chuks. Two hardwood sticks tied together with a two inch chain. Considered a deadly weapon, they are used by karate weapons people.

Perps. Perpetrator, one who commits a crime.

Quadrant. A quarter of a circle. Used on the side of your knife, it represents half of a half circle. Different quadrants have different functions and are used to measure different things, such as time, or vertical distance, or linear distance down a mountainside.

Quillion. The part of a hunting knife that separates the handle from the blade. We drilled ours so it could be used as a peep sight.

Trued. Shaved while turning around so that an arrow is straight and even.

Two knuckle hold. Index and forefinger on either side of the blade and slightly to the rear of the clip. It's used when unzipping an animal's hide, and again when opening the peritoneum. It keeps the point of the knife from making a hole in the carcass on the side of the knife away from you.

Triangle sides. Named for trigonometry according to where they are located with reference to the angle **measured**. The second angle is always square, that is, 90 degrees.

Weight/utility ratio. The ratio of the heaviness of an item to its usefulness in the woods. Plastic ties weigh nothing, yet prove highly useful. On the other hand, a 19" TV + generator rates poorly.

Weighted line. A string, line, or monofilament line that is weighted to hang straight and down. When the line is motionless, it will indicated any angle to which your knife points, either up or down.

EVERYBODY'S KNIFE BIBLE
INDEX
(with important illustrations in **bold**)

A

B

C

KNIFE PUBLICATIONS

If you want to know the best about anything, read more. Other knife publications not only keep you informed with the latest and greatest, but some contain ads from various manufacturers featuring the hottest knife deals and the latest products.

Because you bought this book, **you're entitled to subscription discounts.** Call or write for subscription rates: From those rates, discount the following amounts: From the regular subscription rate, take your discount and enclose the balance in payment. Quote discount by referring to *Everybody's Knife Bible*, from Path Finder.

Knife World. **$5. discount.** Write: 730 N. Broadway, Knoxville, TN 37917. Published in newspaper tabloid form, these people know what they're doing. It contains articles for the collector, as well as articles on knives for special uses. They list books for sale on nothing but knives, and always publish an excellent classified section containing some good deals. Listings and locations for knife shows appear regularly.

Blade Magazine. **$2. discount.** A slick magazine sold all over the country. They hire writers who know knives and feature all kinds of articles. Highly respected in the trade, they feature knifemaker's and manufacturers' ads coupled with a directory which feature the latest creations. They also feature ads for Jantz and other suppliers of make-it-yourself kits and supplies for home knife crafters. Write: Blade Magazine, 6237 Vance Rd., Suites 1&2, Chattanooga, TN 37421.

Knives Illustrated, **$2. discount.** McMullen and Yee Publishing, 2145 La Palma Ave, Anaheim, CA 92801. This is a succesful quarterly debating now about becoming a bi-monthly publication. They feature knife writers and review anything to do with knives. Many issues feature step-by-step know how on knife construction.

OTHER, WORTH WHILE, RELATED PUBLICATIONS
American Survival Magazine **$2. discount.** 2145 La Palma Ave, Anaheim, CA 92801. Top rate magazine. They give survival a wider definition than most. Therefore, the magazine contains useful information for anyone who wants to live. What's out there that might hurt you? Whatever it might be, this magazine covers the problem and provides the solutions. Last year, for example, they ran articles on special survival knives, AIDS prevention, and several good firearms.

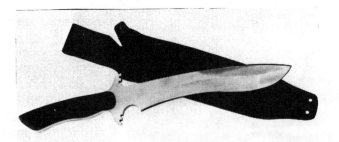

The Mamba, by Blackjack. The company made big reputation on this model. Handguard is user- friendly. Choil on blade gives control. Knife comes sharpened forever by factory. Lower blade curvature gives super cutting effect.

Kukris. Lower blade curvatures make cutting edge entry easier.

Trailmaster. Cold Steel. Highly touted blade by Alaskan hunters. This shaves hair right out of the box. Pommel hole is important.

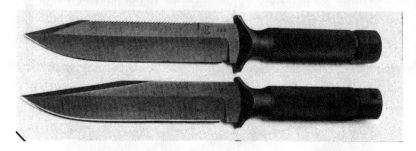

Hollow handle knives are made from one piece of steel. Normally, you have to add goodies to the handle package.

Gut hook on the back of this Schrade blade opens things up as if using a zipper. You need round-rod to sharpen one.

TEAR OUT OR COPY THIS PAGE
USE YOUR PRODUCT REBATE COUPONS JUST
LIKE CASH WHEN YOU ORDER FROM PATH FINDER

Path Finder's product rebate coupons (reverse side) can be used as cash at most of our dealers or by mail order from Path Finder Publications on any of the following:

NEVER GET LOST. P.A.U.L. system. The Green Beret's Compass Course. Reviewed by almost every major outdoor magazine, this book contains your land navigation system of the future. You can go anywhere, anytime, **without a map**, and never get lost. We've sold over 25,000 of these and have hundreds of testimonial letters.

Price before coupon discount: **$9.95**

EVERYBODY'S KNIFE BIBLE. First reviewed by the *AMERICAN SURVIVAL GUIDE MAGAZINE.* They called it "innovative, funny, and sixteen of the most inventive and informative chapters on knives and knife uses ever written." This is **the book** to own if you want to perform like a woods-king in the outdoors with your knife.

Price before coupon discount: **$12.95**

AMMO FOREVER. Total self sufficiency for every gun you own. By Huber. June 92. Simplifies reloading for all gun types. When the government shuts off supply, this book will keep your guns loaded.

Price before coupon discount: **$12.95**

EVERYBODY'S OUTDOOR SURVIVAL GUIDE, The Green Beret's Guide to Outdoor Survival. Over 15,000 in print with great reviews. This book teaches you survival arts as if you were on a Green Beret team. Best shooting instruction around for all weapons. It has Woodcroft's hand-to-hand combat methods, water purification. Also, how to double your survive-ability with help from animals, plus more.

Price before coupon discount: **$12.95**

GREAT LIVIN' IN GRUBBY TIMES, The Green Beret's Guide #2. No other book ever taught weapons selection for survival like this one. It has combat shooting and the legendary Brian Adam's ESCAPE AND EVASION plus too much more to mention. We've sold over 10,000.   Price before coupon discount: **$12.95**

THE COMPLETE SELF DEFENSE MANUAL Huber. Covers ways and means to protect yourself and family. Takes defense by time frame, before, during and after attempted crime. Weapons, range, tactics, and more.   **$14.95**

These are your discount checks.

They work just the same as cash when used to purchase from Path Finder.
*DEALERS. We accept customer coupons from you as reverse keystone value cash on our books.

FROM: _____

_____ ____/____/____
_____   date

Pay to the order of: Path Finder Publications // $2.50
        Two dollars and fifty cents_____

For: BOOKS   _____

FROM: _____

_____ ____/____/____
_____   date

Pay to the order of: Path Finder Publications // $2.50
        Two dollars and fifty cents_____

For: BOOKS   _____

FROM: _____

_____ ____/____/____
_____   date

Pay to the order of: Path Finder Publications // $5.00
        FIVE dollars --------------------------_____

For: Merchandise   _____

Mail to:

Path Finder Publications

1296 E. Gibson Rd., Suite 301 Woodland, Calif. 95695